Talk to Me
What the Dead Whisper in Your Ear

Allison DuBois

an Allison DuBois Book
Published by STTT, Inc.
Phoenix

STTT, Inc.
1500 West Warner Road, Suite 200
Gilbert, AZ 85233

designed by Joseph DuBois

First edition June 2011

For order inquiries please contact STTT, Inc. sales at
602-501-1994 or service@allisondubois.com or visit:
www.allisondubois.com

Manufactured in the United States of America
1 3 5 7 9 10 8 6 4 2

ISBN-13:   978-0-9761535-1-1
ISBN-10:   0-9761535-1-3

Dedication

This book is dedicated to my grandmother, Jenee (Genevieve) Parrack, who passed away in 2010 at the age of 93. She had the most beautiful blue eyes and a sweet tooth like no other. She always said, "Allison, Heaven won't have me and Hell don't want me!" She was one of a kind. We love you, grandma. I'll miss your cackle.

Our prayers go out to the lovely people of New Zealand and Australia. Many of you have been challenged by Mother Nature recently and you persevered.

Also, to the people of Japan, who have endured such great devastation due to the tsunami and earthquakes that have shaken your foundation. Joe and I have many friends in Japan, and they are truly some of the kindest, funniest people we've ever encountered. Our hearts go out to all of you. Please know that we care deeply.

Table of Contents

Foreword

"What's it like to be married to the Medium?"

Those are often the first words I hear when I am introduced to someone new. I hear it enough that I figure the chances are good that you have the same question, too. Before I get to the answer, let me tell you a little about this book, because the two topics are entwined. To read this book is to get to know Allison better, for she shares her personality in her own words, her own thoughts, her experiences with the living and yes, the dead, too.

In this book, Allison recalls some of the many people she has met during the course of her seminar tours and personal readings. Each time Allison conducts a reading she accepts some of the living person's grief. In order to do this, she must connect with the deceased and die a little herself. Allison takes these experiences and connects them with a greater theme that everyone can relate to. Some are inspirational; others help with personal growth or self-awareness. Allison has such a unique perspective because she is a medium. Not only does she assume the perspective of the person who has died, she also has the perspective of the healer who has seen many ways to move through grief and see a bigger picture. By sharing these stories, Allison tries to process out what she has experienced. She must do this in order to let the energy go; otherwise, it continues to take a toll on her, as each reading has permanently changed her.

Allison provides her perspective to each reading, yet there is another version, too. There is also the story of the living people left behind to pick up the pieces. Allison has invited some of the people whom she has read to include their experiences in their own words. She also shares the words of the deceased who has passed on. The family of the deceased has spent a life-time with each other, so they are able to apply the specific message to the full story of the decedent's life and validate Allison's information.

I feel that I can provide yet another facet by answering the question, "What's it like being married to the Medium?"

As Allison's husband, I have a unique viewpoint. I am her closest confidant. I am there for it all. I see her like no one else does. I see the depth of many readings and the common arc of the story that they tell. I see how Allison is affected and grows and changes after each reading. I see how she needs to be brought back to the land of the living and process out all of the grief she has absorbed. It's quite a process she goes through—very emotionally taxing.

The first time that I heard this question was in 2005, just before *Medium* was to premiere. Allison was scheduled to attend a press junket in Los Angeles to support the new show. Our life had changed quite a bit in a short time, so there was a real chance that we would get overwhelmed. Up until that point, our life fit snugly in the suburbs. I went to work from 9-5, and Allison interned at the District Attorney's office. Our three school-aged kids were involved in cheerleading, volleyball, etc. We had barbecues on the weekend with our friends.

Oh, yeah, there was that other thing—the way my wife had this uncanny ability to pick winning juries and detect motives and know who has committed a violent crime and when a suspect will turn over to open up a case. Like in the Natalie Holloway case when Allison went on CNN and said that she "sensed" that Joran Van der Sloot, a suspect in the disappearance of Holloway, would start bragging and sharing details of the crime in two years. That's exactly what happened. It unleashed a media storm of strange press interviews with Van der Sloot where he continued to provide details around a "murder," and then ended up retracting what he had stated. Van der Sloot had also told an acquaintance of his a version of what happened that fateful night in Aruba, who then went to the authorities with the details.

There were also many instances amongst even the little DuBois females in our family, like the way my daughter would talk to my deceased father or scare her friends by telling them about the little girl ghost hanging around their house. But for the most part, we maintained a typical suburban lifestyle.

Then, seemingly all of the sudden, we were flying to Los Angeles for publicity. It was so surreal.

To deal with the added stress, we came together as a couple. She had a job to do to promote the show. She was thrust into the spotlight for all to see, with her abilities sometimes drawing unfounded controversy. I would like to go on about some of the less reputable press and their true lack of intelligence and impartiality, but that would just be for my own gratification. My point is merely that there was a lot of stress put on Allison. Of course, I took her side and traveled to Los Angeles to provide her with both physical and emotional support. I have since found that this type of support is a recurring theme. Being a public figure isn't as easy as some think.

Since the show was Allison's project, and I was there in more of a support role, I was hoping not to be asked any questions by the press. The show, of course, is named "*Medium*," not "*Guy Married to a Medium*." I knew that was wishful thinking, so I tried to think of questions that I might be asked. If I had the answers all ready, I could hopefully prevent my natural instinct to ramble. I had thought the first question would be, "How is the show different from your real life?"

When we showed up to the hotel where the event was being held, there were celebrities everywhere. We were introduced to a journalist, and after he finished his interview with Allison he turned to me.

I thought, "I'm not nervous. I'm ready."

Here it came, the first question: "What's it like to be married to the Medium?"

I guess the two questions are similar, except that the question I had thought of was less personal, more objective, more aloof and calculated. The question he asked was more emotional, more all-inclusive, open-ended, and definitely more subjective. What were they looking for in this question?

I stumbled, cleared my throat and said, "Wow." I was trying to take a little time to think. I ended up saying, "We were very young when we got married, I really don't know any other way."

At least I didn't ramble. I also didn't really answer the question. It was more of a shuck and jive.

The thing is, I certainly have stories to tell about our daily life that make our life different. That reporter does, too. When he got back to the office and played the tape recording of the interview, everyone's voice was clear, but Allison's sounded like it was being played backward. That's kind of funny the first time it happens, but after the 4th cell phone, or the unknown number of camera batteries sucked lifeless, it starts to become expected.

Some things are easy to describe and to know that they are not the norm. For instance, when Allison would catch our daughters in little white lies regarding getting into the cookies, or when Allison was waiting for our daughter outside her bedroom window as she tried to sneak out. Fairly simple things like how Allison, or for that matter all my girls, can "know" what their birthday gifts are going to be when it was supposed to be a surprise.

Some things are harder to capture, like how she can sum up a person relatively quickly. So quickly that it seems like the person just left a bad first impression on her. In the beginning, Allison might share with her girlfriend that her new boyfriend is creepy or seemed "off" somehow. Of course Allison's girlfriend would be newly "in love," and not want to hear this, so she'd get quite offended. In return, Allison would know what she knows and feel like the friend did not respect her advice, and shouldn't have asked her at all. The friendship would end and a few months later Allison would get a call, "You were right, I'm sorry."

The first time that happened it was hard to mend the relationship. For that matter, it is still hard to mend some relationships. When someone asks her for her help and then doesn't like the answer, what do you do with that?

Some things take time to get used to. Like driving. I usually do the driving, which has become an art of the avoidance. Since Allison does sum up people rather quickly, she is affected by all of the other drivers around us. There may be one she does not want to be near, and since her personality is that of a race car driver, she always wants to be in front rather than let the annoyance pass by.

Allison has a very compassionate heart for those truly in need and an absolute abhorrence for those working the system. I have seen her go out of her way to feed the homeless. I am not talking about the money we donate to charity, or even the time she spends volunteering at charity events, but actually buying a hamburger in a drive-thru to personally give to someone in need. She has given the jacket off her back to clothe the needy. At the same time, she has no time for people who are merely working the system. I think she learned this from her Grandpa Joe. He was the same way. She believes "you never take more than you give."

Some things are unexplainable. I have to keep a lot of spare light bulbs on hand because they always mysteriously break in my house. I have found that during fits of anxiety, teenage girls have the greatest power of breaking light bulbs without touching them. They also have the ability to freeze computers, snap crystals, drain batteries and otherwise affect modern life. I do not have conclusive evidence, but the weather also seems to follow Allison's mood.

One of the most perplexing happenings was when I was

driving Allison and John Edward (who is another world-renown medium) to dinner. As soon as they got into the car, it turned off. It just shut down. All of the electronics simply turned off. It had never happened before and it has not happened since. The car otherwise worked perfectly and turned right back on when I turned the key off and then on. That was quite a night. Later on, John's cell phone died. I mean it really died. He lost all of his contacts, and I think he still blames Allison for that, in a playful way of course. The most interesting part of his phone dying is that it sat on the dinner table for 45-minutes or an hour, with the light on, but it would not fully turn on to become functional. John fiddled with it and put it down several times. Allison mentioned John's mother in the conversation and the phone made a noise and then powered off for good.

We have been married long enough that I can't always tell what experiences set us apart from others and what things make us like every other couple in the world. In some ways I have it easier because Allison can read my mind. I don't always verbally share my feelings or thoughts because she already knows them anyway.

Isn't this how many people feel when they're in love . . . the other person finishes their sentences, or perfectly acts as their counterpoint? I think you can understand why I first fell in love with this beautiful, complicated woman.

At first it seemed like I had it harder because Allison was reading my mind. When I got upset, I couldn't hide it. If I disagreed with her, it would never come across politely because she could "feel" my uncensored vibe. Even now, I can't conceal my emotions from Allison, let alone if she outright asks me if her shoes match her dress.

It took some time for me to figure out that her picking up on my vibe is really a benefit. She can read my mind, and she married me anyway! It is a very freeing feeling learning how to really share what we all hold inside. I now live my life as though it is on the front page of the newspaper, and that's okay.

In some ways the question about being married to a medium is similar to being asked what is it like to be married to a redhead. I have done some research and found that redheads really are different. It has been discovered that redheads require 30% more anesthesia to be sedated. Redheads bleed more. Redheads have a higher pain tolerance and in fact, redheads have a stronger libido. Not only have these traits been observed, the underlying, genetically based science has been discovered. I found these facts to be so interesting that I wonder what other differences they might have.

I would not be surprised if Allison's psychic ability is related to the same genetic trait that gives her red hair. Wherever the psychic ability comes from, it is only half of what makes her unique. The other half is the strength of her personality. She has a very good sense of who she is. This strength in personality allows her to use her ability and not let her ability use her.

Allison has a public personality that is compassionate, yet tough as nails, and she is true to herself. She is tenacious and not afraid to fight if it's for something she believes in. One thing that I think people do not understand is that just because she can fight, doesn't mean that it doesn't hurt when she gets cut.

This book may be the real answer to who Allison really is The words that follow are written by Allison, not by a ghostwriter. She opens up her heart and shares how she feels and is affected by each reading. You will catch a glimpse of the genuine Allison DuBois. And since we are all human, you may also catch a glimpse of yourself, too.

-Joe DuBois
April 12th, 2011
Los Angeles

Chapter 1

How Spirits Talk to Me

"For those who believe, no proof is necessary. For those who don't believe, no proof is possible." – Stuart Chase

Spirits communicate in various ways. Some ways are easily dismissed by most, others are not so easy to dismiss. I wrote this chapter so you'll take a second look the next time someone tries to get your attention from the Otherside.

Have you ever seen light out of the corner of your eye, and when you turned it was gone? It's usually a sharp, bright spark that doesn't look like anything you've seen before. Don't dismiss it or make an eye appointment. It's spirit letting you know they're watching over you. It's most likely a relative of yours checking in on you, so just say "Hello" and continue on with your chores. Sometimes spirits will appear as a shadowy figure trying to stay back in the shadows to be around you, but are trying not to scare you at the same time.

I know shadowy figures may seem scary initially, but

maybe they won't be now that you know they're appearing in that form to be sensitive to you by trying to blend in with the background. Once they know they're "wanted" there, they communicate in other ways with you that, in my opinion, are less creepy ways. If you feel a presence around you and feel fearful, sometimes it's just an entity trying to warn you about a family member who's about to pass or someone close to you who's needing immediate medical attention.

When I get one of these "visits," I pay real close attention because it can be a window for me to intervene for someone whom I care about. Often a picture of a person we know will flash in our mind, and if it erects a feeling of illness or something dark, then you can see that as a warning flag. People who have passed away will attempt to save us from an upcoming catastrophic event, and if that means going through a friend of your friend because they're the most open, then they'll do it. So, it's essential to understand your inner voice, because sometimes that's the deceased's only way to reach you. So, learn to speak their language and they'll help you to interpret what they're telling you.

If you're really lucky, you'll get a "visit" in a dream from someone you miss, letting you know they're all right and still with you. If they aren't smiling, don't assume they're mad at you. Often they appear solemn until you begin to acknowledge that it's really them, and to truly see how hard they've worked to get through to you out of their love for you.

Have you ever had your breath "stolen" from you where you're forced to take a deep breath for no apparent reason? This often happens when you walk through a spirit who already occupied the space you moved through; it's usually in a hallway in your house, but it can happen in other areas as well. Most of the time the spirits that stay around you just want to be recognized as an active part of your life. Once you acknowledge their presence, they usually step up their game because they know you're open to communicate with them. You may find that the spiritual activity around you becomes stronger and more obviously them.

If you're open to interacting with the Otherside, try getting a "feel" for whether they're female or male. Women have a warm feeling to them, a maternal energy; males have a cooler essence, more masculine, solid. Do they feel eye-level, or does the energy feel centered closer to the floor (meaning that it's probably a child)? Is it a familiar feeling? Does it feel like someone you recognize?

If you can identify them, then communication becomes immediate. Tell them what you need to know from them and how you feel when you're around them. Don't challenge them to levitate a refrigerator or throw a table across the room. It's insulting to them, and since they're emotionally based beings, they'll tell you to "go pound salt." However, you can ask them for signs that will be clearly "them," specific to their personality.

They'll answer your questions. Just be careful to not let your mind override your soul sense too much, or you'll dismiss all of their signs. This frustrates them when they try so hard to give you what you need. Keep in mind they're emotionally based energy, not intellectually based. They won't come through with a code word, but they will make sure their information really hits home with you and is unmistakably specific to their personality.

When I connect with the deceased, I like to use a pencil and pad of paper and write impressions down of how I feel, or any images that pop into my head, or what I hear being said, or other things like that. Use your senses, be open, and raise your energy level. They want to communicate, or they wouldn't be there with you. I think it's so spectacular to think that the people we lose can choose to be in any time, place, or with others who've passed on, and often they choose to stay with us because we're their version of heaven. I mean, really think about that . . . they find you so special and extra-ordinary that you are their ideal. I love that!

Those who pass seem to share some common feelings. People who were physically alone when they died, or their loved ones weren't there to say good-bye when they died, tell me that they were never really "alone." Family and friends who pass before them surround them at their time of passing to take them quickly. We are so good and fast to blame ourselves for what we "didn't" do for the deceased, often failing to recognize what we "did" do for them. When spirits come through, it's often in an attempt to alleviate our guilt so that we can re-join the living and stop dismantling our lives.

The living also get hung up on "not" getting to say good-bye. The deceased are quick to point out that there are no good-byes; they don't want the relationship to end. From their point of view, it's confusing as to why it's so monumental, this word, this act of good-bye. They're in it for the long haul. They're not wanting or ready to leave, and we also don't have the power to hold them here through our grief. It's a great misconception that we're somehow "hurting" those we love by suspending them in time with us. They stay because they want to, not because they're energetically bound to us through our sadness. Get that? It's their choice to continue forward with us. You're not leaving them behind; we carry them with us because they're part of us, and that can never be changed.

Signs

I had been approached by a charity organization called the New Foundation. They were putting on an event that was a "Dancing with the Local Stars" fundraiser. They asked if I'd participate and I agreed. I figured I'd do it as a tribute to my dad,who was a professional ballroom dancer. He had always wanted me to follow in his footsteps, but I was a competitive skater and had no interest in changing sports. I decided to perform the last dance that I saw him perform for competition. It was a Samba, and he danced to the song "Copacabana." So there it was, my chance to dance for my dad, and I knew he would be there to see me. While taking lessons, my partner Rik was so patient with my lack of attendance and my very hectic book tour schedule, but quick to remind me of how out of shape I really was. I tried to channel my dad when attempting to dance without stepping all over my partner's feet.

In August of 2007, I was pulled to a place called Lily Dale that is outside of Buffalo, NY. I was looking to center myself and get in a better frame of mind and maybe even relax a little. I took my own advice and made time for myself, even though it wasn't convenient. I knew it never would be. While I was on my flight from Phoenix to Buffalo, I was reading an uncorrected proof of my book *Secrets of the Monarch* to prepare for my press tour. I was deep in thought reading Chapter 8, "Coping with the Loss of a Parent and Learning How to Reconnect with the Dead." The pilot's voice came over the intercom, and boy he had a great sense of humor! So he was telling us jokes, and then he broke into song. He changed some of the words to fit Southwest airlines, but he was singing to the melody from "Copacabana." I grinned from ear to ear. I found it so uplifting, it was just what I needed. I smiled, I knew Dad was with me, and this was a sign that many people might have overlooked, but I knew better than to dismiss such a wonderful gesture.

So anyway, I arrived in NY and I was in the car on my way to the hotel. After a restless night's sleep under a full moon and a lunar eclipse, I was up, dressed and finally on my way to Lily Dale. Yeah! As Debbie, my host, was driving me up a winding road, I looked to my right and saw the house number 222. This is another of my dad's wonderful signs, since he died on the 22nd of '02. I talk in detail in my books about "222" being his sign to me, reassuring me he was still in my corner. I called my husband, Joe, to tell him of the fantastic signs that I'd been receiving. He shared that a fan on my blog with the call-name "Copacabana" wanted to know if I was going to be in Lily Dale that weekend. Well, that was icing on the cake, and I knew my dad was telling me he was giddy about my dance tribute to him and that he was around me keeping an eye on my performance.

People always ask me about signs. They want to know how to recognize the signs from their loved ones. I impress upon them that you have to learn to pay attention to what your "inner" voice is telling you. There is something intensely intuitive inside of us all, and it is as powerful as any sense that we can possess. We don't need our eyes for this kind of recognition, you don't hear it with your ears, you can't touch it with your hands; you just know it in the same way you first know you love someone. You know it because a force within you holds onto you and won't let go. You'd recognize the presence of a loved one even if your eyes were shut and they physically are no longer here. Even to the point that you feel you need to speak their name out loud to validate them. They love this because they know they're "getting through" to you after all.

There are so many great signs, and some are definitely harder to read than others. At one of my events, I had a mature yet handsome man raise his hand to ask a question during our Q and A. He wanted to know why he's always seeing the number "13" on clocks. His eyes are drawn to it when "13" appears, and also he has a daughter born on the 13th. It's everywhere for him.

I usually like people to figure these sort of signs out by themselves, but as Joe points out, I sometimes forget the task I hand back to them can't always be accomplished without having abilities. I could feel it was a "mother figure" connected to the man asking the question. So I said, "It's got to be mother or grandmother giving you the sign."

He said, "My mom's still alive and I don't know why my grandmother would do it. Maybe it's my grandfather? We were very close."

I shook my head "No." "The presence isn't male, it's female."

He looked puzzled and said, "I don't know why my grandmother would need to let me know she's with me. We weren't very close, and she died when I was thirteen."

The audience was amused and taken aback, understandably so. The gentleman and his daughter smiled at one another and he appeared touched by his grandmother's efforts to let him know that she never left him.

It's important for people to keep in mind that it's not about what we "want" them to say or whom we want brought through; it's on their terms because they're running the show. If they have energy on coming through, they'll find a way. They are emotionally based beings, so their messages are motivated by their feelings for you, not always your feelings for them. Just because you didn't know a family member in your lifetime doesn't mean they don't know you. They watch you grow up and they form an affection and love for you as if you were interacting with them on a day-to-day basis. So be careful not to deny a loved one based on your limited experiences with them. It never hurts to have a large family rooting for you to succeed in life, even if their life has already been lived.

Tucson

While visiting our friends in Phoenix, Arizona, our friend Duffy showed us her phone, and it had an application called "Ghost Radar." Joe, being science-minded, thought it was cute, so he downloaded it to his phone, as well. It looks like a radar on your screen. When there's activity around it, words pop up on the screen, and I mean random words. There may be a few words an hour on a good day.

So Joe and I took off for Tucson for my next event. We never really know what kind of people we'll have at my events, since different cities carry various energies. The Tucson event was predominantly "loss of children," so afterwards I was quite tired.

After I exited the stage, Joe pulled me aside. "Allison, it was the craziest thing. During the event my Ghost Radar was going crazy and the word "Mark" popped up on the screen. How random is that?"

Why this was so strange is that my cousin, who helps me at my events, is named Mark, and his dad passed the year before, so I had no doubt that was his father's way of letting him know that he was there.

Cool, huh? Spirits can manipulate electronics, so why not? We've had many creepy yet cool messages from this application since then, but that's the one that stopped me in my tracks.

We've not received another name on our "Ghost Radar" since my Tucson event.

San Antonio

When you travel on tour with somebody as often as I traveled with my cousin Mark, you get to see someone close to you deal with their own personal daily trials and tribulations. This includes how they're affected by death and the daunting task of trying to become familiar with it. Mark struggled with his personal loss of his father while trying to keep the shows together as we bounced from city to city trying to help others work through with their own pain. Here's my cousin's interpretation of his own sign from above.

Mark's Story

It was February, and this was the month that Allison's Family Connection Tour was not only taking us to Texas but to San Antonio, the city my father was raised in, the city he loved.

My dad's name is Juan Antonio Hernandez. He was born in San Luiso Potosi, Mexico, but later grew up in San Antonio. He passed away at the age of sixty-nine from Alzheimer's on April 4, 2009. He was known to his friends and family as Anthony, Johnny or Juan, answering to them all. My father loved music, dancing and dressing nicely. I remember him talking about singing in the church choir when he was an altarboy, as well as going to all the Sock Hops as a teenager, and as he would put it, "dance the night away." To this day I can visualize his shoes lined up in his closet, glowing in a dark closet because of their shine. I can picture his shirts neatly pressed and his suits all lined up in order by color. Needless to say, if there was soulful music and dancing, my dad was always dressed to perfection.

One of my father's favorite artists is Neil Diamond. I can remember many mornings as a young boy waking up on Saturday and Sunday to Mariachi music or Neil Diamond playing on the stereo. My dad so loved Neil Diamond that he took me to four of his concerts during my youth. His favorite song was "Sweet Caroline," and he's the reason I'm a huge fan of Diamond's music.

As we were driving from Austin to San Antonio, I couldn't help but remember the time when my dad showed me the photographs of a visit we had made to San Antonio when I was a toddler, but I felt that this was truly my first trip there, since I don't remember being a toddler. San Antonio was the third and final city on our February tour, and after a week in Texas, I was really excited and so looking forward to communication from my dad. I didn't know exactly what sign he would send me, but I did know he would make himself present on the visit.

Obviously, I felt very connected to the city because of its special meaning to me. I found myself being so drawn to the River Walk, and even though I had my back to it, I was constantly being turned around and felt fixated on the view. It got to a point where I could tell Allison was getting frustrated with me because she didn't have my full undivided attention, which happens from time to time when cousins work and travel together on the road. LOL. Allison asked for the bill and in my head I said, "Thank God," because by now it was even starting to bother me that I could not stop gazing outside at the River Walk.

We both went upstairs excited that we were getting ready for our last event. As usual, the event went well, and Allison and I headed to the hotel bar to decompress. Our decompression sessions usually consist of a few cocktails and Allison and I discussing the readings. We do this because it is very common for Allison and me to get sick if we don't release the energy from the event through conversation.

After our discussion, Allison stepped outside on the patio and later returned with a biggest grin on her face that I've ever seen. She wanted me to join her outside because there was a group of men playing and singing music on the same patio that I had been drawn to earlier. As I walked out onto the patio, I had a feeling that something magical was about to happen. I saw the musicians. They were Hispanic, dressed in tuxedos and enjoying life as they sang and swayed from side-to-side beneath the moon. After the first song ended, the gentleman in the group with the guitar asked me what song I'd like to hear. I told him "Sweet Caroline," not knowing if he could play the song or not. These guys weren't musicians the hotel hired, they were businessmen who brought their instruments with them because it's their hobby, so I wasn't sure what to expect.

The guitarist began playing and all I could say was, "Thank you, Dad."

I wanted to say thank you to my dad because even though he had sent me signs since his passing, for the first time, I really knew that I was truly communicating with him and that he was listening to every request I had. I thanked him for being a great father, for molding me into the person that I am today, for still being with me, guiding and helping me to raise my two boys as he raised me.

The next morning, I left San Antonio feeling like I had the first vacation with my dad in his new life. I will never forget the trip, and I have been playing Neil Diamond music for my boys since, and guess what their favorite song is?

Coincidentally, as a footnote, Allison and Neil Diamond have the same birthday, too. Nice.

Chapter 2

Heart and Souls

Joe is the love of my life and the father of my three beautiful girls. When the television show *Medium* toyed with the idea
of Joe dying and leaving us, it shook me to the core. It also inspired me to write this chapter and to dedicate it to all the
people out there who lost their love far too soon. If you're lucky
enough to have a person in your life who makes you feel more
alive than you ever knew was possible, hold them often and
never take them for granted because there are no guarantees
for tomorrow. I hope this chapter makes you want to go do
something nice for someone you love. If it does, think of the ex-
ponential good that has come out of learning from loss.

Paul and Janeta

While I was touring Australia, I read a young woman
named Janeta at one of my seminars. She had endured a lot of
pain, a pain that most of us never experience. Still, she wasn't
bitter or resentful; she was a very special lady trying to stay positive as she pieced her life back together. When she learned

about her life-changing loss, she was 5-months pregnant with her son. The person she had lost was her husband.

I can't imagine the thought process she went through wondering how she was going to describe to her son how wonderful his dad was and what an aneurysm is—this thing that ended his father's life. When somebody like Janeta crosses my path, I am so grateful to be able to sit with them and try to walk them through the darkest days of their lives, so they can come back into the light of the living. Here's Janeta's account of our reading.

Janeta's Story

In 2004, I met my soulmate, the man of my dreams and the love of my life. I fell helplessly in love with him and I couldn't live without him. I thanked God every single day for blessing me with such a great love, and I truly did feel lucky and loved by God. My husband and I were inseparable. We did everything together and we had a really good relationship and marriage. My family adored him, as he was such a good-hearted man. He was handsome, athletic, a hard-worker and very humble. My husband and I planned on having a long life together and growing old together. The thought of living my life without my husband was something that I could not fathom. He was my life, the air I breathed—he was my world. We were expecting a baby boy, so we were at the very core of our happiness. We were both on top of the world and as my husband always said to me, "We have our entire life ahead of us."

My husband died when I was five-months pregnant. He died of a brain aneurysm, so his death was sudden and unexpected. I wasn't home when he passed on, so the fact that he died alone plagued me for some time. After his death, my sister gave me Allison DuBois' book *Don't Kiss Them Goodbye* to read, and from the very first page I was hooked. From that moment on, I wanted to know everything there was about the Afterlife, so I was forever reading.

I looked up Allison DuBois' website after reading her books, and sent an email to her manager asking whether she'd be visiting Australia anytime. I was so excited to receive an almost immediate reply advising that she had, in fact, planned to visit Australia the following year.

True to her word, she did travel to Australia in December 2010, and I attended with my sisters. We were seated near the back, as it was raining heavily and we were stuck in traffic. My first words to my sisters after seeing the crowd and the location of our seating were: "There's no way I'm going to get selected, no way!"

When Allison came out, everyone was so excited. I was amongst them. For nearly a year, this woman had helped me more than she could possibly know, and finally, I was able to see her and enjoy her company for a couple of hours. Most of the readings were conducted from where the people were sitting, but she did ask some people to join her on stage. I was fortunate enough to be one of those people.

When I was selected, I first thanked Allison for the books that she had written, as they had helped me to understand "death," so to speak, in a completely new way. Allison taught me, through her books, that my husband's soul or spirit continued to exist after his death, and that we would meet again when

I passed on.

When I was on stage with her, I was completely over-whelmed. Not only did she look angelic, but the crowd was over-whelming me, too. There was literally a sea of people in front of me.

My husband came through right away, and the first thing he said was: "I'm sorry."

I guess he was sorry for dying and leaving our baby boy and me. He reassured me that he loved me so much. In the reading my husband referred to a necklace I had purchased after his death. He said it was a locket and then he stated that I had placed his photo inside of it.

Allison described the necklace to me exactly. She also told me that my husband has met my son and kisses him good-night daily. He also said that he "tucks me in," and Allison said that he sometimes sleeps on his side of the bed, so I was told to "keep to my side!"

In the delivery room, when giving birth to my son, I felt Paul's presence and I thought I heard him say something to me. I was heavily drugged, so I thought that maybe I had imagined it. In the reading Allison told me that my husband was present at our son's birth, and that he had given me a message that day. This confirmed to me that I hadn't imagined his voice or his presence—it really did happen. He was there to see the arrival of his much anticipated baby boy.

Allison referred to the balloon my son had sent his daddy on the one-year anniversary of his death. She even said that Paul had gotten the message that was written inside the bal-loon.

That was unbelievable, because there was no way that Allison could have known that, unless Paul had told her. She also mentioned that my husband was present when my son had his photo taken with Santa Claus. This had occurred about three days before Allison's event, and I did feel my husband's presence on that day.

Allison told me that my husband was sorry that we didn't have the family we planned to have, but he told her that I was going to have a baby girl one day. I was shocked at that piece of information, as I never thought I'd find love again, but Allison reassured me that my husband said that I would.

As I indicated above, my husband died alone, and I had many unresolved feelings that had been weighing on my mind. Allison told me that my husband didn't die immediately, but rather, was unconscious and passed on peacefully. That made me feel so much better knowing that he didn't suffer. I always believed that if I had been home, that I could have saved him, and we could continue on with our life. Allison told me that it was his time and he would have passed on regardless of my having been home or not. I guess that made me accept that you cannot get out of death. When it's your time, it's your time.

Allison said a lot more to me that night, but I was so overwhelmed by everything that I have chosen only the main things to write about. I think she is an amazing person and she has given me so much hope that my husband and I are still connected and we will reunite one day. She is truly gifted, and I thank her for all that she has done to help me in the most terrible time of my life.

Jim and Dot

Unlike Janeta, Dot was with her husband when he died. Her husband, Jim, had a terminal illness so they knew the day was coming. I thought an example of both knowing ahead of time, and losing somebody without notice, would be food for thought for you to weigh the pro's and con's of both scenarios. For all of us, we will die one way or the other, with or without notice. There are no in-betweens. I think by looking at the two very different ways to lose a loved one, it can cause us to recognize how essential it is to value life. We can see life in a profound light so that we don't miss one single opportunity with someone we love. Here is Dot's account of our meeting:

Dot's Story

I had heard about Allison DuBois, and I decided that I wanted to attend one of her events, so I ordered the tickets online with the support of my husband. Of course, he would not go to the seminar with me as Jim just really did NOT believe in all of that sort of ethereal stuff, so to speak (at the time). I selected the VIP ticket for the early meet-and-greet, and I got the books that Allison had written when I checked in so I could ask her to sign them.

Allison was sitting at a small table, and each person was allowed a short one-on-one greeting, and then Allison would sign their book. When it was my turn I, placed the books on the table in no particular order and asked her to sign one book to my husband Jim, another one to my friend Suzanne who was supposed to be with me that day, and one of the books for me. I did not ask her to put a particular name on any of the books specifically, as I was not even familiar with the books. I then told Allison I knew when there is a TV series or movie that is based on real people, many details are changed to make them fit the time-frame of the show. I told her that I had seen on one of the episodes of *Medium* (the show based on her life), that her character "Allison" could see the number of days a person had left to live when she wore certain white sunglasses. I asked her if anything like that was true. Allison stated she saw it more as a "gas tank."

Early on, the very beginning of Allison's talk, she informed the audience there would be a portion of the evening when she would take life questions, and then a portion when a few people from the audience could come up to the stage and she would do a short reading for them. You could tell Allison was a very nice, kind, compassionate person. She let us know that when she did the readings, to understand that parents who have lost children hurt the worst. She stated she was sure that everyone there in the audience had probably lost someone, and if they had an okay ending with their loved one, to understand that parents who have lost children would really benefit from a reading if they could get one. She then went on to tell us that she did not see visions in her dreams like the TV series portrayed; she got her information while she's awake, so not to worry about her going into a weird trance or anything.

I really was not sure what a life question was, but I knew I wanted to ask how long my husband had to live. Even though he was feeling well at the time, I just had to ask that question. I had hopes he would live ten years, but I wanted to be realistic—

after all he had pancreatic cancer and the statistics were not
that good.

I was able to ask her about the length of life for my husband, and she wasn't sure; she only knew that March was
pivotal for him and me both. On the way home, again a long
two-hour drive, I called my sister and my friend relaying to them
what had happened, telling them I asked her how long Jim had
to live. We noted she did not say how long he had to live, but
that March would be a pivotal month. I took it for what it was,
since it was not a one-on-one reading (when Allison concen-
trates directly on a particular person). Again, I took March as being a pivotal month for what it was, did not really know what it
meant, but thinking it could mean he could get much better or it
could mean he would get much worse. At least, this is how I
took it at the time. So, I got busy planning a family trip for good
times.

After the event, I decided I needed a private reading with
Allison. At the seminar in February, I signed up for a private
reading. The sign-up sheet was a legal size sheet of paper and,
of course, the list of names was long. They told us that at some
point Allison's assistant would call and set up the reading.

I guess about one month passed and I missed a call on my
cell phone while I was at work. I am a Registered Nurse and I
have worked in the Operating Room for over 20-years. I returned the call It was from Allison's assistant, and he had set the
date when Allison would call me for a reading on the telephone.
I asked Allison's assistant if we could do the reading face-to-
face, and he said she really did not have the time to do those
anymore. I was happy to get what I could, so I set the date up.

The date came that Allison was going to call me for my reading on the telephone. I took the entire day off from work. My husband and I went out and bought a brand new phone that was not a portable phone because I did not want to have any problems with the connection. We set a place up in our bedroom that was quiet. I had a writing tablet, a writing table, and Jim seemed happy for me as he knew this was something that I really wanted. Although he said he did not believe in all of that stuff, Jim was a pretty open person and supportive any interests that I had. He also respected my intelligence enough to know I would not be wasting my time or be so enthusiastic on a wild goose chase; he was mentally taking notes.

Allison was to call me around four o'clock, and her assistant called a little later than 4:00 and told me that she had been delayed. He said the reading she did prior to mine took longer than expected, and she would need 30-45 minutes to rest. Allison did call about the time that her assistant stated that she would. She was apologetic for not calling at the prior arranged time and, of course, I indicated that was okay. I understood she was tired from her prior reading. I asked if she wished to do mine another day as she was tired, and she said, "No, it's okay."

I reiterated another day would be fine, and would it be possible for us to do this face-to-face? I would really rather conduct my reading face-to-face.

She asked why I would rather have a face-to-face reading.

I told her that I have always preferred important conversations to be face-to-face.

She said that I would have to wait a couple of months before she could do a face-to-face, in-person reading, and I was fine with that.

About a week later her assistant called and we arranged the meeting, two months into the future. The meeting was arranged to be in Arizona, and I proceeded with travel arrangements to include our family for a little vacation.

Throughout the month I thought about what I wanted to talk to her about, but I did not start my list until we got into Arizona the day before I was to see her. The time finally came for my appointment with Allison. My pad in hand with about three pages of notes, I was invited in by Allison, and we sat down.

I asked Allison if I would be okay emotionally and financially after my husband passed away. I also asked her if I should quit my job to spend time with Jim.

She said," No, no, you need your job."

I said, "Well, Jim was wondering if he should go back to work.

She said, "Oh no, if he goes back to work it will be the same as if you were taking your child to work with you each day. You will be spending all your time checking on whether or not he's taking his medication, if he was eating, etc.; it would be harder for both of you."

I just have to say that when Allison gives answers to life questions, she is very accurate. The exact was true even when my husband stayed home and did not work. I had to make sure he ate and took his medication constantly.

So again, I asked Allison when she thought my husband would die. I told her that at the seminar in Austin, she had said March was a pivotal month, and I figured that meant that March 22 was what she was talking about. That is the date my husband and I were married in the church. We were not born Cath-olic, we chose or "were called" to be Catholic, and quite honestly glad we became Catholic. There are things in and about the Catholic Church per say, that we do not agree with, and I think probably most people in religions are that way. I am okay with that. Jim was never too much into the rosary, but it certainly nev-er kept him from loving being Catholic. My point is that it was very significant that March was a pivotal month for us, and it was, actually, pivotal for our family, too. Our entire family was Catholic. His three children from a previous marriage are Cath-olic, I became Catholic, and then my children did, and then Jim did. We sent our kids to Catholic school up until high school. I think I understand that no one really knows when someone is going to die, except God. But I asked Allison if she had an idea and she said, "What I can tell you is that November will be his sickest month thus far." My reading was June 25, 2010. I asked her if she thought he was going to die in November.

She said, "No, he will not die in November, but it will be his sickest month. "

I told her that I hoped he would get well, because I had a trip planned for Hawaii December 19. She scribbled on her pad and said, "Don't buy the tickets!"

I said, "I already have. I bought them in May. I had to buy them ahead of time." I told her I already paid for the condo, too. She told me to see if I could get a refund.

I said, "Well, you know, if he is just going to be sick, I figure we can put him on the plane and take him around to see the beautiful places on the island, and have a good time. At least he would be on the vacation with us and we could have the experience together. "

She said he could make it but it, would be very, very hard on him. Again, my reading was June 25, 2010.

In September we went to MD Anderson and my husband's lab values were better. His CT scan was better. His PET scan was better. Everything was better. October his lab values went up a little bit, not too bad. He was still feeling good. All went well through October and at the end of October his lab values were up a little bit. We had an appointment at MD Anderson the first couple of days of November. Jim's CA 19-9 had gone up, and Jim's oncologist and Jim agreed to change the chemotherapy treatment and put Jim on some that was a lot stronger. This made Jim very, very sick.

The month before he had won the Victoria Country Club First Round Club Championship in golf. Now, all he could do was sleep, and he did not feel like eating at all. He had not lost his hair up until now, either. He was proud that he had cancer for over one year and received chemotherapy and never lost his hair. Now, in November he started losing his hair, pretty much lost his self-esteem, and stayed in bed most of the time, often with a fever, and then sweating after breaking the fever. He started losing weight, as he could not eat very much. He just couldn't eat.

We went back to MD Anderson for another dose of chemotherapy. One week later his CA 19-9 had gone up 58%. The chemotherapy was changed again, another round of four different kinds of chemotherapy, one by mouth and the other three by IV. Jim was sick, sick, sick; he did not feel like playing golf, and did not feel like getting out of the house at all. At one point, he even said if this was living then he had to talk to the oncologist because this was not living. He did not feel like talking on the phone. He did not feel like having visitors. December the 8th was his birthday, and I did not want the day to go by uncelebrated, for I knew this would be his last birthday on this earth. I wanted to have some kind of celebration. He was feeling a little bit better, so at the last minute I had some people over.

Allison also brought my mother through for me in the reading, and my mom gave me some wonderful messages and details of her life to re-live.

Then Allison said something else I really did not know about, someone named "Grace." I made a note about someone named Grace connected to my mom whom she was with now, so I could look into that when I left. My mom also mentioned a coin collection that I was unaware of.

Later, I told my sister, Shirley, about what Allison said about dad's coin collection, and Shirley said she had some of his dimes, but really did not know much about a coin collection so to speak. She also said that he had some Kennedy silver dollars, though neither one of us really knew what he had and could not remember if the Kennedy heads were half-dollars or silver dollars,not that it mattered. I asked my sister about Grace, and she said there was a lady named Grace Woodard who mother used to have coffee with every morning when we lived in Refugio when I was little. So that made sense that Grace was with my mom. They were probably gabbing and having coffee together.

I told my husband about the answers that Allison had responded to me with about my life questions, and my husband seemed interested. I talked about the coin collection that my mom had mentioned. Actually, I had talked about the coin collection a few of times in front of Jim, and he did not say anything about it, no comment.

Then one day we were sitting in the backyard, and I called the father of a friend of our son. His son, our son's friend, had been murdered. I told him what Allison had said during my reading, and I told him that she was coming to Chicago and I wanted to make sure he would go. He said "No,"he was sending his daughter, named Allison, in his place.

I said, "No, Greg, you need to go because she talks to parents who have lost their children first."

So he did decide to go.

I told him that Allison had told me two things that did not really make sense to me. One was about a lady named Grace, and my sister did tell me that my mother used to have coffee with Grace Woodard every morning, and the other was about a coin collection. I do not really remember a coin collection.

My husband, Jim, was sitting outside with me when I was telling Greg about the collection, and Jim stands up and says, "Dot, I have the coin collection."

I said, "What?"

He said, "I have the coin collection," and he walked into the house.

I said, "Greg, he says he has the coin collection and I have no idea what he is talking about!"

Well, a couple of minutes later, Jim walked outside with this medium to large bag that is kind of beige in color, like you would see on the Monopoly game. It was a bag filled with coins and dollar bills, lots of coins that I had never seen before. A lot of those Kennedy half-dollars or silver dollars, a lot of dimes, coins from different countries, all kinds of coins—and a lot of them. Dollar bills and envelops of two-dollar bills, and I mean a significant coin collection that I did not even know existed!

I said, "Jim, where did this come from? Where did you get it?"

He told me that after my mom had a stroke and we were getting sitters to come over to her house to stay with her, that's when he took out all the rifles and guns from my dad's closet. He took that bag of coins and had left it where we keep the guns all this time.

About a week later my husband said, "You know, I might talk to a medium sometime."

I said that I thought that was a good idea.

Then he said, "But it could only be Allison DuBois."

I said, "Oh God, Jim, you can't talk to Allison DuBois, you have to go to a seminar first, and then you have to sign up and wait to be called for an appointment."

Then he said, "I have to talk to her in person."

I told him that she doesn't do face-to-face sit-downs! Mine was just a stroke of luck. Anyway, I started the process of emailing Allison's assistant to see if she would see Jim. To make a long story short, things happen because they are supposed to, and are directed from places beyond our control. Allison did agree to see Jim.

In the meeting, she told Jim that he was the second person whom she knew to have pancreatic cancer, and the other person was her father-in-law whose name was also James. There you have another connection that is not just a coincidence.

My husband is a most private man and does not feel close to a lot of people. A lot of people feel close to him. He is a kind and compassionate OB-GYN, and it is not uncommon for women to feel close to someone who takes care of them during that period of their lives. However, Jim does not share his feelings or expose his emotions to anyone. After 24-years of marriage, I was honored to have some exposure to his innermost feelings. Dealing with this cancer was the most difficult time he had ever had in dealing with anything. He was scared and uneasy about death.

Many friends asked if he was "okay with the Lord." The answer was of course, "Yes," but that does not get someone ready to die, especially someone who loved his life on this earth and had five children and a lot more living to do. He still had not walked his daughter down the aisle. He had golf tournaments to win, grandchildren to get to know and, of course, more time to make important relationships better. He was just not ready to check out.

Before seeing Allison, I would say Jim was ill at rest about death. Not only was he not ready to check out because he enjoyed life, he just did not seem comfortable about it. He would say, "I hope I have been good enough." And believe me, he is golden—more than good enough!"

Allison met with Jim on September 10, 2010. I had gone out to get my hair done and do some shopping. When I returned to our hotel, I have to say that Jim was the most peaceful, calm and content I had ever known him to be. After some asking, Jim shared with me that Allison described his dad and their dog and some experiences they had, and about a letter that was written.

Jim said Allison also talked about a grandfather who was coming through to him. Jim said in her "scribbling" she kept making dollar ($) signs. Jim said he had to chuckle because ever since he had to stop working we had been getting royalty checks from gas wells that his grandfather had long ago sold the land on, but retained the mineral rights to. So, the dollar signs made perfect sense.

Jim said he did not directly ask Allison how long he had to live. He did share with me that Allison said he would be able to make what he called my "birthday trip" to Hawaii, but it would be very, very hard on him. Jim said they shared a nice parting hug when he left that made him feel pretty good.

November was a hard month for Jim, but then he seemed to be feeling upbeat a few days before our trip to Hawaii. On the night that we boarded our flight Jim felt nauseous. The same would hold true for the following day; he still did not feel like eating. We had driven to Houston Saturday and spent the night. Saturday night he had a bowl of onion soup. Sunday morning, the 19th, he felt good. He had a couple of bowls of cereal and milk.

Later we boarded our plane, stressed out and running late. Two hours into the flight my husband started throwing up. He told me he thought I was going to have to take him to the emergency room when the plane landed in Honolulu. From the plane I called a surgeon whom we know. He told me, for sure, to take him to the emergency room in Honolulu. The surgeon said he was concerned about an obstruction, something not uncommon after a Whipple procedure which Jim had a year earlier. Jim threw up again one more time. Jim said, "Let's just go on to

Maui and get the kids to the condo and see how I do."

We were there for one day. Jim was trying to feel good. The next day he felt terrible. We went to the emergency room in Maui that night after midnight. It had great doctors who offered to do some things, but Jim said he just wanted to go back to Victoria because he knew he would really get the best care for himself there. That morning, around 5:00 am, I was making flight arrangements to leave Maui to get back to Houston and drive to Victoria. We left Maui around five o'clock December 22nd, and got to Houston at six o'clock the next morning.

A few weeks later my heroic husband passed away on the 22nd of January 2011.

Thank goodness the Sunday before Jim died, I had gone to the nursing home where Jim's mother lives and brought her to the house to see him. She is "with it" if you talk to her one-on-one. If you have three people in the room talking at the same time, she gets confused, but still pretty "with it."

Even though it was late when Jim passed away, I told the kids to go to the nursing home to tell their grandmother about Jim's passing. It would be better for her to hear it from them. Jim is a well-known physician in our community. I would hate for someone who got there the next morning to say, "Oh Mrs. Hayes, I am so sorry to hear about Dr. Hayes!" before we had the chance to let her know personally and process it with her.

The kids went over to the nursing home at about 10:30 that night to tell Jim's mother that her son had died. They found out that Jim's sister had been there that day and moved her to Dallas. Allison had warned me that this would happen seven months prior, so I think it helped me cope in a time when I needed all the help I could get.

Allison and I had talked about how death sometimes makes people do insensitive things, but at least I knew ahead of time what to expect so I could roll with it. I'm taking it day-by-day, I know Jim's around me, and that he's feeling good again. I miss our talks and sharing our highs and lows from our day. I miss being part of a couple, but I will carry him in my heart with me through life, so I guess I'm not really alone after all.

Meeting Jim

Now that you have read Dot's account, I want to share with you how her reading affected my life.

When my cousin Mark called and told me that Dot wanted to book a reading with me for Jim, I initially said, "No."

I said no because I bring through the dead, but I was being asked to counsel the dying, and that petrified me. What if Jim didn't like me or couldn't get past his scientific background in medicine? What if I said something that made it worse for him? This wasn't my forté; it was unfamiliar ground for me.

On top of those fears, his name was "Jim," and he had pancreatic cancer, just like my father-in-law, the one I never met in life. Could I handle it? Our daughter, Fallon, was born five years to the day that my father-in-law, Jim, had died, and I saw Joe still struggle with losing his father. Part of me wasn't sure that this wouldn't affect Joe, seeing a man of similar age, name, and illness pass through our home and our lives. Or maybe it could help Joe to process his father's passing, something he had never entirely been able to face. He missed him so much. I spent weeks thinking about this, weighing the possibilities.

Fortunately, my cousin Mark is very smooth and he's able to talk anybody into just about anything, and he did. In spite of all my reservations, I agreed to read Jim and set my fears aside. After all, he was dealing with a time issue here, so now was not the time to lose my cool.

Jim came over on September 10th, two weeks before the anniversary of my own dad's passing. I had many conflicting emotions raging through me.

I noticed that Jim had the kindest blue eyes, and he's one of those guys you look at and KNOW he's a doctor; he exudes the energy of a doctor. He sat down and we talked for a few minutes so that I could put him at ease. This was, after all, a unique situation. We talked about what happens when a person dies, how they can reconnect with the living, and how they can still participate in the lives of their loved ones. This seemed to calm his nerves a little bit. As the reading progressed, he seemed more and more at ease, and even seemed amused by the information that was coming through from his family in the reading.

I razzed him, "See, it doesn't hurt a bit! This is a completely painless process," and we both snickered.

I brought through many relatives and described their personalities and gave him names and other details. The more I conveyed to him, the less stressed he looked. I felt a bond with him for many reasons. It was a most precious experience, one that has changed me. Now I know that I can help the dying, too!

I was so afraid to face that fear, to feel his pain, his very life slipping away. But then I realized it really wasn't slipping away; it was simply changing forms. I also felt so honored that with Jim's limited time, he chose to spend part of it with me talking about life and death. Talking about his wife and kids and how much he loves them all, savors every conversation with them, every moment. When we were finished, I hugged him good-bye wanting to hold on to him and keep him here, but it doesn't work that way, does it? I know we all wish it did.

I saw Jim six weeks later. He looked different. He had lost some of the color in his face, but he still looked happy. He was still amongst the living. We were at a fundraiser, for what else? Pancreatic cancer research. We had a lovely, yet emotionally draining evening. He and Dot stopped by the next day to drop off their T-shirts for our family from their favorite football team, the Texas Longhorns—such a sweet gesture.

January rolled around. It's my favorite month because I was born in it!

January 22nd was a Saturday, and it was on the night of my birthday party that Jim let go. I remembered back to when I met Dot, and I kept seeing the number "2" connected to Jim. Then I found out that they were married on the 22nd of March, my dad passed on the 22nd of September, and now Jim on the 22nd of January. What a guy! He delivered babies all those years witnessing life coming in to this world. It made sense why death and life exiting the world didn't feel right to him, because it's not what he knew.

Days after Jim passed away, Dot told me that Jim had told her that the meeting with me made it so he was no longer so afraid to die. To hear these words was just one more life moment that made my life profoundly worth living. People often ask me what their life's path is, and it's nice to know that each of us has the capacity to touch others' lives for the better. If we all tried just 10% harder to help others, think of what a wonderful world we'd leave as our legacy.

"Jim, thanks for the memories and for pushing me to be better at what I do and how I live!"

Jill's Parents

While writing about those who have to endure the excruciatingly painful loss of the love of their life, I also wanted to show my readers the flipside of loss, the reunion.

Although one half of a couple often will pass away first, the day does come when they're reunited, together forever. Occasionally, I have the unique honor of bringing an inspiring couple who has passed away through for their family, and the dynamic duo speaks of their unbreakable bond, their life together as they walk hand-in-hand down memory lane. In this case death brings them back to life, because once again they have each other.

I conducted a 30-minute reading for a woman named Jill. She missed her parents terribly, having lost both of them at such a young age.

I knew nothing about her parents, but I was on the verge of finding out why these two people were so special to Jill and her entire family, and why she needed me to reconnect her with them.

The relationship with our mom and dad is one that can't be replaced or forgotten—it's one of a kind, unparalleled. When I bring somebody's mom or a dad through for the kids, I take it very seriously because I'm fully aware of how precious those relationships are to all hearts involved.

I wrote "MOM" and "DAD" down on my pad of paper, and I drew a line from those two words to Jill's name trying to grab one of her parent's attention, and within seconds I could hear her mother begin whispering messages for Jill. So, I brought Jill's mom through first, since her mom had quite a strong need to reconnect with her daughter, and her dad was politely letting his wife go first.

Jill's mom felt very warm and was chatty. She started off by acknowledging the little boy and girl saying that she felt connected to them, protective of them.

I said, "This is either a set of her kids or grandkids."

Jill responded with, "My sister is pregnant with twins, a boy and a girl."

Her mom sadly referenced "the female with cancer" being strongly connected to her.

Jill informed me that her mom had passed from cancer.

"That's your mom's way of acknowledging her illness so that you know that it's gone now. She's healthy once again."

"Jill, your mom says she rides in the new car."

"Allison, I just bought a new car two days ago!"

I love moments like that where the communication is so crystal clear from the Otherside that the living are totally taken aback because it's so specific to their everyday life.

Jill's mom talked about her albums from the 1970's and how she wanted them to be played and enjoyed. Jill confirmed having a big box of her mom's records from the 1970's.

Her mom spoke of a flower garden and the color pink and the desire for her daughter to plant that garden so they can still have their private talks.

Jill then told me that her mom had a rose garden and that she would plant one, too, for their "private" talks.

Then I asked Jill's mom to step back for a moment so that I could pull Jill's dad through.

"Jill, your dad shows his name being times two, meaning there's someone who carries his name as a middle name."

"My brother's middle name is Tim, after my dad."

That was Tim's way of showing that he's still around his namesake, his son. Jill's dad was really sarcastic and full of life, and he laughed about the T-shirts that his wife couldn't stand him to wear. He wanted his daughter to have them. She informed me that they had a box of his "forbidden shirts," and she had made a quilt out of them. I think that was a brilliant way to honor her dad, a fantastic idea.

Then her dad talked about a dog, and I asked Jill if she knew of a dog named "Buffy."

Jill was a little stunned, and then she shared that they have a dog that they love very much named "Buff."

Jill's parents showed me the two of them bowling, and they said that they were on a bowling league together. Jill confirmed this, too.

Jill's parents are much younger now, and neither of them have cancer anymore. They still adore their children, and they will watch over their little grandchildren all the days of their lives. It was a loving and light-hearted reading, reminding us all that we'll forever be in the arms of those that we love.

Jill's Story

My sister, brother, and I were very lucky to have two wonderful parents! I had a great childhood and was very close with my mom and dad. We had a family full of honesty, trust, a lot of laughter, fun times, and an abundance of love. My mom and dad were high school sweethearts who were hard workers; yet, they always made time to have fun and enjoy life. My mom had a very positive attitude and could see the good in any situation. She was very friendly and loved people. She could talk to a stranger for hours if Dad would let her. My dad had a way of making the person he was with seem like the center of his world, whether it was me doing homework with him, or a client in his office. He had a great sense of humor, and anyone that knew him, would tell you how sarcastic he could be. Because of his job, many people saw a stern, powerful person and didn't have the pleasure of knowing who he really was. Unfortunately, my parents were taken from us too soon, leaving much sadness, many questions, and a huge hole in our family.

Within the first five minutes of my reading, Allison commented that I was a very pragmatic person. This is very true, and I also tend to be quite skeptical, so you can imagine that grasping the idea that I could talk to loved ones who had passed, and that they could talk to me, was difficult to do. I was a huge fan of the show *Medium*, and the real Allison Dubois peaked my interests. I read her books, and after each one, I was more convinced that there was at least a little truth behind this.

In April 2010, I attended one of her seminars in Denver. I had read on her website that she would pick just a small handful of people at her conferences to do a personal reading. The excitement of hearing a message from my mom and dad was very thrilling, but I knew that it was a long shot that I would be chosen. At the seminar before Allison spoke, her assistant explained to a large room full of people how her readings would work. People would be selected based on how "loud" the people on the other side were, and the stronger spirits would determine who would be chosen for a reading. Allison then asked the crowd who would like a reading, and I raised my hand along with almost everyone else in that room. You can imagine the shock when I was the first person chosen. I said a quiet "Thank you" to my folks for being pushy.

Allison spent about 15-minutes with me, passing on messages from my parents. This skeptical, pragmatic person left that night on an emotional high, now convinced that there was some truth to this and that my parents were with me. Before I left that night, I signed up to have another personal reading. More than a year passed before I had the second reading.

It took Allison's books to open my mind, and her personal reading to convince me. But it took the second reading to actually listen to what my parents were saying. I consider myself extremely blessed to have the opportunity for a second reading to actually process this evolution.

In both readings, Allison started off by saying that my mom came through right away and talks A LOT. That's my mom, the talker! Allison knew nothing about me, my parents, or the way they passed, but apparently Mom was filling her in. Allison said my mom was talking about the female with cancer, and asked if either my mom or my mom's mom had passed from cancer. I lost my mom to brain cancer when she was only 54. Later, when speaking with my dad, she said that he wasn't revealing how he died; he wasn't telling her anything. However, she could see that he was holding his chest like he was in pain, or was having a hard time breathing, and that he might have had a hand in his death. My dad passed away from lung cancer at the age of 55. He smoked, and he felt a lot of guilt and remorse for smoking, even though he knew the risks. Cancer is a very cruel monster that disrupted our lives and caused us a lot of pain. It doesn't surprise me that they found it important to connect to me by discussing, or not discussing, their cancer. Allison assured me that they didn't have it anymore and that they were healthy. I needed to hear this.

Allison said that my parents were both presenting themselves at a younger age. She said my mom was beautiful with very long hair. She was indeed beautiful and had very long hair. She was presenting herself at the age of 23, and said that was a very good year for her, filled with joy. I was born when she was 23. Furthermore, she said my dad was presenting himself at the age of 25 because it was such a happy time. Again, that was his age when I was born.

One of the first things that Allison said Mom kept talking about was the boy and the girl, and she explained that that usually meant either she had a boy and a girl, or there would be a grandson and a granddaughter. My sister is pregnant with twins —a boy and a girl. Allison said that my mom was acknowledging them and wanted my sister to know that she would be there with them and act as protection for them. She also said Mom was referencing May, and that there was a strong family tie to the month of May, either a birth or a passing. The twins aren't due in

May, but my sister's doctor told her that twins usually come early, and that they could be born in May. Also, my mom passed away in May.

I don't wear much jewelry, but the jewelry I do wear has a special story or meaning behind it. Allison told me that my mom was talking about the two necklaces and a ring. My parents gave me a ring for my college graduation. I wear it all the time, and I think of them whenever I look at it. I also have two necklaces that I take turns wearing. I remember one morning I put on my diamond necklace. Later that day, my parents called me with the news that my dad had cancer. I made a decision to keep that necklace on until my dad got better. Several months later, that necklace broke and later that day, my dad's doctor told us that there was nothing else he could do for my dad. That necklace had been a symbol of hope for me, so the irony of it breaking on the day the doctor's were giving up was remarkable. I believe my mom was letting me know that she knew my jewelry has an emotional connection to my parents.

When Allison was speaking with my dad, she said he kept saying his name times two. She asked who else in the family had my dad's name. My brother's middle name is Timothy, after my dad. She said that he was trying to acknowledge my brother, and that was his way of doing so. She said there was a strong tie with my dad's shoes, and asked if my brother had a pair of his old shoes. At first, I took it literally. I don't know if my brother actually does have a pair of my dad's shoes. But I think that could be interpreted figuratively, too, and it couldn't be more dead on. My brother idolized my dad so much, and he has stood in our dad's shoes, having chosen the same career path. My dad was a journalist, and my brother works for the same newspaper that my dad worked for, and is constantly saying that he is proud to follow in dad's footsteps, and hopes he makes him proud. Allison told me that Dad was saying my brother wouldn't "get" this process. I had told him about my first reading with Allison, and my brother didn't believe it. The fact that my dad pointed out my brother's skepticism let me know that Dad was there for our conversations.

My dad had been gone for six years, and my mom four years when Allison first read for me. We thought we had resolved any remaining issues regarding their estate, but Allison told me that my dad was saying that there was still money tied up in the estate that hadn't been dispersed. Three days after the reading, I got a letter from the State Controller's Office regarding an unclaimed account of theirs. We are currently in the process of recovering that money.

I was very close to my parents, and when I moved out of the house, I talked to them on the phone a lot, especially my mom. It's been five years since my mom has been gone, and every now and then I find myself thinking, "Oh, I need to call Mom and talk to her about..." and then quickly remember that I can't. Allison told me that my mom missed talking on the phone and that Mom would be messing with my phone to let me know that she was around. About four or five times a week, our phone rings with a weird sequence of rings. There is no rhyme or reason behind this, and it is completely random. It doesn't happen when certain people call, or at a certain time of day. I hung up the phone with Allison after our second reading, and later that afternoon the phone rang with that familiar, obnoxious ring sequence. Rather than being annoyed by it as I usually would be, I smiled and I thought of chatting on the phone with my mom.

Holidays were always special in our house, and we had many traditions. Every Easter for example, we would decorate eggs together. The night before Easter, after we kids went to sleep, my dad would go outside and hide the brightly colored eggs. We lived in the mountains, but no matter how cold and snowy it was, he would go out in the dark and climb around hiding those eggs for us to find the next morning. It made me smile when Allison said that my dad loved Easter and all of the activities involved with the holiday.

My parents also always made a huge deal out of birthdays. For one day, the world revolved around you and anything you wanted. My dad always only wanted one thing: German chocolate cake. Somehow it didn't surprise me when Allison told me that my dad was telling her how much he loved sweets and cake especially on his birthday. But not just any cake, it had to be a special cake. Allison was seeing a marble or chocolate cake. I knew exactly what she was talking about.

Allison described my dad very well. She said that he came off as being very tough, but would bend over backwards for us. She also chuckled and said he was very sarcastic. The way she explained him further reassured me that she was indeed seeing my dad.

After I graduated from high school, my parents moved from the mountains of Colorado to the sunny weather of California. The selling point of their new house was the rose bushes in the back yard. The yard was filled with flowers, and my parents spent many hours in their backyard taking care of their roses. I almost got tired of hearing about those roses whenever I would call. Apparently my mom is still talking about her roses. Allison told me that she loved her rose garden and told me to plant some roses for her.

We always had dogs and cats growing up, so it wasn't surprising that Allison told me my parents were surrounded by pets. She also told me about seeing my dad with a dog with white, curly hair. But when she told me she saw a dog named Buffy, my jaw dropped. Our family's dog's name was Buff, and he had light, light tan curly hair. I still get shivers when I hear this!

I'd say it's uncanny the similarities between the two readings, but I realize that she visited with the same two people and saw the same thing. It's just like if I were to visit a couple down the street and went back a few weeks later, I'd see the same thing.

Both readings mentioned identical things... Mom said that I was a very stubborn person and that I needed to let my guard down; that Mother's Day was important to my mom and that it was important to honor her with flowers; my parents saw me as 7-years-old; and that I was not going to die the way she did or suffer the way she did. Both readings also really emphasized just how in love my parents were. Anniversaries were important to them, and they love each other now as much as ever. My mom knew what a heavy burden it was with her leaving, and she said she was sorry. In both readings, Allison said she could see my parents leaning up against a jukebox. She spoke of my mom's love of music, especially '70's music. They were hippies in the 60's and 70's, and we always joked about how terrible their music was.

In each reading, Allison told me that my parents like to ride in the car with me. This doesn't surprise me. When they were alive, we spent a lot of time "just driving," a long-time family joke about the number of hours our family would spend in the car out for an adventure of some kind. As similar as I was to my parents, a major difference between us is our political views. I listen to a lot of AM talk-radio, and my husband always jokes with me that my parents would be so disappointed in me. So, I had to chuckle when Allison told me that although they liked riding with me, they didn't like what I was listening to on the radio. In the second reading, Allison told me that they were talking about the new car, and she asked me what they were talking about. Just two days earlier, I had gotten a new car.

My dad really enjoyed movies, and it didn't surprise me when Allison mentioned this in both of her readings. He loved renting movies and watching them with the family. He almost took offense if we didn't sit and watch his movie with him, and it was a running joke in our family. My dad couldn't believe that I had never seen "It's a Wonderful Life," and every Christmas he would urge me to see it. The busyness of the Christmas season would always take over, and I have yet to see the movie. Even after his death, my dad found a way to nag me about that movie. Allison told me that Dad was once again telling me to go rent "It's a Wonderful Life," and he wanted me to know that that's what he and my mom wanted for my life.

Allison told me that my dad kept referencing his old T-shirts, some with logos, and that they annoyed my mom. My dad loved his T-shirts! He had quite a collection of shirts, including many from Hard Rock Café's across the world. There were several shirts that my mom called his forbidden T-shirts, and she would refuse to go into public with him if he wore them. After my dad passed away, I made a quilt for myself and each of my siblings, and in each quilt, I included Mom's forbidden shirts. My quilt means a lot to me, and even more after hearing my dad talk about his annoying shirt collection. Allison said Dad was still wearing those shirts, and I'm sure Mom is oh, so pleased.

Throughout the readings, Allison kept telling me that they were so in love with each other, as much now as ever. She said that they hoped that I could have what they had. My dad wanted to make sure that I was treated right. That was his concern when he was alive, so it doesn't surprise me that he still says that.

Allison said several times that my parents just wanted me to be happy. She also said that my mom said not to be so hard on myself. I have always struggled with that, so it was helpful to hear those comforting words. After the reading, I was telling one of my friends about my parents' wishes for my happiness. I had never heard this story, but my friend told me that while my mom was sick in the hospital, my friend went to visit her. During that visit, she told my friend, "All Jill's dad and I want is for Jill to be happy." I am happy, Mom and Dad.

In the readings, Allison was able to pass on many facts about my parents, which is what this "pragmatic" person needed to hear. But above and beyond that, she brought through their personalities and their hearts. They were kind-hearted, free-spirited, and loving people. They always wanted the best for us kids. They liked to live every day like it was the last, appreciate what you have, laugh, and love those close to you. That was and still is my mom and dad. I have so much peace knowing that they are still "living" that way today. I am proud to have carried on many of the values that they instilled in me. They taught me that life is short; don't forget to stop and enjoy life. I hope to honor them and learn from them and live each day of my life with the outlook that they both had.

Chapter 3

Spirits and Children

Every seminar on my tour carries a "theme." Sometimes it's predominantly "loss of father," other times "suicide" will be the majority of the readings. This isn't planned; it's just how it works. The Otherside draws together people who have common energy, who carry common pain.

When I was in Texas in 2010, I had a three-city tour in a four-day period. I found the three cities had something in common more than sharing a state; all three events had a heart-wrenching theme: "loss of children."

I always ask my audiences to reach out to one another during my events and console their neighbor if they feel inclined to do so, because we are all connected and should be that shoulder-to-cry-on when we can. One of my events was in Austin, Texas, and the people were really friendly, but as usual my life gravitates to the news, and this was no exception. My manager/cousin Mark and I were traveling from Houston, Texas, and the national headline of the day was that an airplane had flown into an IRS building in Austin.

I turned to Mark and jokingly said, "You don't suppose that was next to our hotel do you?"

Well, as it turned out, it WAS, and the media circus and police presence were so fierce we couldn't even get to our hotel. We had to take a crazy detour and pass right by the burned building. The sight of it made one grateful to be alive, as we stared at the black hole that was the cancer on the building where a day ago the buzz of every day life had been. Helicopters hovered like birds around the crime scene. The town was in disarray, and I only hoped that the next night would be calm for my audience who had already been rocked to their emotional core through their own losses. Fortunately, everything worked out just fine, and the ballroom began to fill up on the night of my event as I saw my usual excited, nervous line of people at my book-signing table one-by-one sharing their time with me. By the way, I have some REALLY good-looking fans, and I mean that's on the inside and out—really quality people.

So anyway, I finished signing books for the crowd and then I began the show talking about different ways one can die. I asked for the hands of people there for a "murder," and then those who had "lost children." A few hands unfortunately remained, meaning they had lost a child to murder. My manager Mark works the microphone and he seemed pulled to a woman with sad eyes named Gail. She came up to the platform and sat in a chair next to me, I wrote her name at the top of my pad of paper, and she told me that she wanted to connect to her daughter.

For those of you who haven't seen me "read," I automatic write; I put a pencil to paper and "scribble." It helps me to focus my energy.

Anyway, her daughter kept showing me the #17, and it wasn't resonating with us why that number was so important to her daughter. We continued. The little girl told me that the man who murdered her had a male friend who, during the crime, knew that it was going on. I found this very disturbing. Her daughter kept talking about being around the detectives who worked her case, and how every detective has that "one" case that they never forget or get over—the one they "take to the grave"—and she IS that case for them. Also, to tell them "thank you" from her for working so hard and caring so much.

After the event, Mark talked to Gail and she told him that the detective was actually in the audience that night, and that the detective said that "17" was how many days the girls body was missing. This reading hit me like a cement slab to the face. Gail's daughter was 12-years-old when she disappeared; my daughter is also 12-years-old. It becomes VERY personal to me when I connect with parents who have their kids ripped from them. I have to believe justice will be served one way or another for the innocent. As for the perpetrators, well, we won't go in to that today.

As I brought the little girl through, I would occasionally become distracted by an audience member crying for Gail, or an empathetic heart breaking in time with hers. People ask me why I prefer doing readings for "trauma" survivors. My answer is that I want to help the people whom others stay away from, the ones no one knows what to say to, the people who become a part of this "private invisible club" of people who lose their children and decide to die with them. They're physically here, but emotionally

they need to be resuscitated, understood, heard-out and reminded to stay open to their babies and to also open their eyes
to life, because those whom we lose physically continue to live
with us soulfully.

Michael

I remember meeting Lyman and Sheila for the first time. It
was for an in-person reading. It struck me that if you saw them
walking down the street, you wouldn't realize they had been
taken apart by tragedy. Their energy was so cool and upbeat,
but doing what I do, I could see in their eyes that something was
missing from their lives. That something was their son Michael.

When I book readings, obviously, I don't want details
around the person passed because it taints what I get, and that
makes for a weaker reading. Michael's parent's experience with
me is chronicled below, and I think what they share is the most
important part of what you need to know about Michael. So, as
to not take away from their account of the reading, I'll keep it
brief.

I include the words of the people that I "read" in my books
because you can relate to them, since they've been through
what you have. I find it important to hear from someone who can
understand your pain entirely. For those of you who haven't
been through this sort of loss, I think you can empathize with the
people sharing their stories. In turn, this empathy you feel towards people is as if you're sending their heart a "Get Well"
card. It's a positive exchange of energy from you to them. Also, I
like to give the person coming through center stage, so the living
can better know what happens to us when we die from those

who've been through it.

Michael came through easily enough. He was focused on his family and answering the questions he surely hears run through their minds every day since his passing. He gave the feeling of pressure to my throat and an inability to breathe. I tried to convey this with sensitivity to his parents. How they felt when they passed is often something they need to share in a reading without throwing in hurtful details.

Michael talked lovingly about how "proud" he is to have Lyman and Sheila as his parents and how lucky he was to have them in his life. He was firm about still being part of the family and spending most of his time around them. He gave the name of one of his friend's who knows more about the incident than he's saying, but for legal reasons I did not include it here. He was very fond of his "black truck," and teasing his sister. There were many details shared in his reading, but what it comes down to is that he was able to orchestrate a reading with me for his parents. He needed to reach them badly and Michael moved Heaven and Earth to do so. It's nice to know that our children need to stay connected to us every bit as strongly as we need to hold on to them. We are indivisible by death . . . they are our children and nothing can truly take them from us, ever.

Michael's Parent's Story

Our 23-year-old son Michael passed away May 2009 from what we believe to be foul play. The police came in and determined it "appeared" to be suicide. We should note that no detective was called to the scene. We have a FBI Forensic specialist and her team who has begun to assist us in putting together all the facts, in the hopes the District Attorney will open the case. We are never prepared to have to conduct an investigation on our own. To this date the District Attorney has turned down two separate requests to open a case. So we will wait for the final autopsy report that we commissioned out for, and attempt again.

Michael was a vibrant loving young man with many attainable goals. On May 24, 2009, Michael had lunch with his sister Jordan, and I at our favorite deli in Northwest Portland. I had already had a quick bite earlier and for some reason I felt the impulse to call Michael to see if he'd like to have lunch. Maybe it was just my being a mom and knowing a college student would not pass up a free meal, and I, being a mom, also wouldn't pass up the chance to spend time with my baby. It was a very relaxing lunch. We planned out our upcoming family day, which we do every Sunday. He let me know he would be at his brother Spencer's high school graduation, but that he would miss the graduation party due to work. At one point his sister went inside the deli and Michael quickly wanted to share the plans for her upcoming surprise 16th birthday trip to Disneyland in December. One of our conversations was about Michael's thick black hair that was longer than I would have liked, and as I gave him my opinion on the issue he reassured me that once he finished his lead role in the upcoming independent film he was in, that he would then let me pay for him to get it cleaned up. I share all this because these are not the actions of someone who is contemplating suicide. I don't think I'm alone in that observation. Following our lunch, I dropped Michael off at his apartment, told him I loved him and to have a good night at work, and that I would see him in a few days.

May 25, 2009, I awoke with a lump in my throat and an ache in my heart that not only lasted all day but also was unlike any I have had before. This was our wedding anniversary and the first time that my husband Lyman and I weren't together to share the day. Lyman was attending his nephew's wedding in Oklahoma. I spent the day getting my yard ready for the big upcoming graduation party so that I could at least spend the upcoming weekend with my husband and kids without all the prepping. I was feeling pretty good about being ahead of schedule. But the ache and lump in my throat continued and I kept telling myself "Stop being a baby, you don't even celebrate your anniversary." I kept saying this to myself throughout the day. As the week went on, neither Lyman nor I had heard from Michael. We are a very close family, and a phone call or text two to three times a day is the norm. But we had heard nothing at all from Michael, and he hadn't returned any of our messages. On Thursday we had gone by his college and asked if he'd been seen, and of course, that information wasn't available to us, as we didn't have the necessary form to have that information released. (Parents, please ask your college student to fill out this form—they should have it in the front office.) By Friday we were very concerned, but didn't want to ask around, as we felt that it was important for Michael to have his independence. Friday evening Lyman called Michael's place of employment, and he had not yet arrived at work. After a few more calls like this we decided to call hospitals as well as the police. We requested a wellness check. Once the police arrived, we were drilled as to why we would be concerned They just didn't seem to get what we were telling them when it came to our communication with

Michael. Finally, they went to his apartment and asked us to wait outside and within minutes we had our answer . . . our Michael was gone. We were told he'd been deceased for about four days. This puts us back to May 25, 2009, the day I had the ache in my heart and the lump in my throat. I now believe without a doubt my soul knew that Michael, my baby, was gone.

I have never cried to this degree in my whole life—it was unending. I felt as if someone just ripped my child from my womb. How could this have happened to our family? It happens to other families—not ours. At least that's how we all feel that false sense of security. But somehow, even after his death, Michael has managed to show us that he is still very much around. The first morning after our loss, Lyman had found at eye-level in the closet a duffle bag strap that had gone missing for almost a year. All the kids were aware that Lyman was not happy that this strap was missing. Spencer had borrowed the bag, and the strap never came back. But on this morning, almost taunting Lyman—there sat the strap! When Lyman asked Spencer where he found it, Spencer said he didn't find it, nor had Jordan or I. It just appeared... Michael? During the first year of Michael's passing, we have experienced TV shows freezing at scenes that only have meaning to us, and the radio playing just the right lyric at the right moment. We know Michael has been communicating with us. We may not have heard him had that strap not shown up on that particular morning.

I was looking for books one evening in the bookstore, and there on the shelf were Allison's books. I am a believer that if I open the book randomly and get a message, then it's meant to be for me. Thus, I purchased all three books and read and re-

read them from cover to cover. I knew then that I needed to at least attend her seminar and see what she had to say. And in April 2010 I did just that. I was amazed at the people she brought through for others. I did not get called upon that evening, but I feel Michael's presence daily and I only had one question for him, "Were we on the right track with our private investigation?" And I also felt that because we are such a close family, that Michael would want his dad to be present when he came through.

In May 2010, I thought I would try and at least email Allison's office to get my name on a wait-list to meet with Allison. I knew this could be a long wait, if it was to happen. I received a reply back noting dates she was available for a phone reading. I knew then that I would not want this, and that I would plan to fly to Arizona in October and take my chances at being called on at her seminar. A few weeks passed, and I had it on my to-do list to email Allison's manager, Mark, and let him know of my plans. On May 24, 2010, the one-year anniversary of the last time I saw Michael, I was at our favorite deli with Lyman, and gave no thought of the location or much thought of the date until I received a call from a number I did not recognize. And because I was selling tickets to a cabaret fundraiser event in Michael's honor for the Art Institute of Portland Film Department, I had to take all calls. It was Mark, following up on possibly setting a phone reading with Allison. You guessed it, I never got to my to-do list. I let Mark know of our plan to attend Allison's October seminar, at which point he let me know that she was going to be in Arizona June 25, and that she could do a reading then if I was interested. No hesitation, we were flying to Arizona in June!

June 25, 2010, Lyman and I met with Allison. As nervous as I was prior to arriving, once we arrived all the nerves relaxed. I felt some sort of comfort. Allison was so welcoming, and made us feel as if we were friends from afar just coming to catch up. Allison couldn't make up the things or the personality that was coming through from Michael. He was happy, he had a lot to say. Michael did touch on his death and let us know that he was okay and that he did not commit suicide. He gave a specific name of someone who he stated was a "friend" of his, and that this friend knows something about his passing and is carrying guilt. He spent some time on this subject, and that told us that we are on the right track. What brought Lyman and me to tears during the reading was when Michael said his head was sore, and that he had a hard time breathing before he died. Allison demonstrated this by grabbing her neck as she repeated what Michael was saying. Allison had no idea that the cause of death was due to asphyxiation. Without asking the question, both Michael and Allison made it very clear that Michael did not take his own life. He wanted to talk more about his siblings. From what he shared with us, we can help guide his brother and sister, and I believe this will give us the patience needed to help them move toward some important goals. We asked if Michael was with his godfather (who had passed away unexpectedly just five months after Michael's passing), and he told us through Allison that he was with "Slick." This was very funny to us. His godfather's nickname was "Spike," and Spike's nickname for Lyman was "Sly"— Sly's nickname + Spike's = Slick! And Spike was quite slick personality-wise, too.

Michael was so open, and through all the times I would tell

Michael while growing up that it was so important for him to communicate with others, as he lacked in this area. Yet, on this day he communicated so clearly. I was very proud of him. Of course, we have always been proud of our son. It was just nice to know he found a strong voice. Through Allison he shared the one song that I would sing to Michael and his siblings, as if it were their own personal lullaby: "Somewhere Over The Rainbow."

Michael kept mentioning "Father Iz" and "rainbow." Then, "Father Iz and over the rainbow."

We got the rainbow part, but the "Father Iz" we just weren't sure of until we realized what it might be. We asked if he meant "Brother IZ," the deceased Hawaiian musician, Israel Kamakawiwo'ole. YES! That's what he was saying.

He wanted us to listen to that version, and he wanted us to know he was with "IZ." My husband Lyman grew up in Hawaii and was friends with IZ, so it was nice to hear they were together.

When we got home from Arizona, the same place the missing strap had disappeared, it now reappeared. Lyman's IZ tank top was sitting out in the open. This shirt is always buried in the closet, but for some reason, Jordan dug it out to wear that weekend while we were in Arizona having our reading. We had not shared with her any information about IZ. Michael was telling us "Happy Birthday," and all we could come up with is that in two days it would be his 24th birthday (the number "24" is his favorite number). But because he kept saying it, I realized at that moment that was for us. You see, Michael was conceived on my 21st birthday, and I would always tease him and tell him he was the gift that just kept on "taking." It was an on-going joke that we shared. So here we are June 2010 and he is telling me "Happy Birthday." Other items that took our breath away were when Allison spoke of Michael's "black truck." Michael loved his truck! And how he was spending lots of time with a petite, elderly lady born circa 1920's, who was probably a grandmother figure to him. The lady is his great-grandmother who is 91-years-old. He said he would be waiting for her on the other side when she crosses over. He gave me the ultimate gift . . . coming through in our reading and communicating!

Following our reading with Allison, I smiled so long I thought I would need to get Botox in my smile lines. I haven't stopped smiling. For the first time since Michael's passing I have been able to sleep through the night. I no longer wake up with tears. I can honestly say that I am at peace. Of course, there will always be days that are harder than others, but I know Michael is okay. I know that he is with us daily, and my faith tells me that when I pass he will be there for me. We believe Michael was instrumental in the timing of the call in May, all the way up to the timing of the specific weekend in June that we were read. We will never be able to thank Allison enough for sharing her gift with us. What she does for families is a blessing. I will move forward and work towards writing and passing the "Michael Bill," which will require all states to have a detective called to the scene when a death has occurred regardless of what the Police and Deputy Medical Examiner feel may be the cause.

We hope to be able to now seek justice for Michael. Now we are able to do so with peace in our hearts.

Irelynn

In Houston I met a wonderful young woman named Jennifer when she stepped onto my stage with her request. She softened her voice and said, "My daughter, can you talk to her?"

I nodded and said, "That's what I do, that's why I'm here, I'll bring her through, don't worry."

With that, she exhaled the breath that she had bottled up inside of her, showing some relief to know the reading she needed was going to happen for her. Jennifer's daughter, Irelynn, was four-years-old when she died—just a baby. I began scribbling, happy that I could feel the little girl coming through so strong. "Your daughter keeps showing me Ronald McDonald. Is she connected to The Ronald McDonald House?"

Jennifer nodded in the affirmative. My smile grew wide at how easily a four-year-old who's all heart can come through just like that! And some long-lived beings who died without loving or living, but lived SO much longer than this four-year-old little girl —they're so much more difficult to bring through. I turned towards Jennifer and I said, "She still lives with you, you know. She says she's happiest there with you. She does say her chest had trauma, it hurt. Did she have trauma in her chest area when she died?"

Jennifer nodded, "Yes, her heart stopped and the doctor had to work on her to get her heart restarted. There was trauma to her chest."

"Your daughter is eating birthday cake and says she wants you to celebrate her birthday still, and make it a happy day again. She's also wishing you 'Merry Christmas!' She says she's 'the princess.'"

"She's dressed in a princess costume and she says she likes all of the Disney princesses."

Jennifer then shared that before her daughter passed away, the family took her to Disneyland, and she was dressed in a princess costume.

"That's important, Jennifer, because she's letting you know that was one of the best days in her little life, so that you know she was happy before she died."

Jennifer was visibly moved, and most importantly, she was smiling knowing her daughter was in the room. "Jennifer, your daughter wants to know if she can go play now."

Jennifer nodded in the affirmative and I shared with the audience that the little girl was running around the room playing, so it was time to conclude her reading. The hum of a collective chuckle filled the room. It was very uplifting. Just think, a four-year-old girl was able to raise the energy in a room full of broken hearts—now that's my definition of a true angel!

Jennifer's Story

My name is Jennifer Pruett; I'm a single mother to my only daughter, Irelynn. My life became very empty on December 22nd 2009, my daughter's 4th birthday. Three weeks prior were the worst three weeks of her life, and mine. Irelynn has been battling leukemia since April 18th 2008, from the age of two. Can you imagine being so little and left without the choice of truly being young and carefree?

Irelynn had just returned from Disney World after being with her father and family members for two weeks. When she returned, she didn't seem like herself. She wasn't eating much nor was she drinking, and when she would eat she couldn't keep it down. She was sleeping a lot, and understandably, very cranky, as well. So unlike my funny, playful, outgoing little girl. November 29th Irelynn was taken down to ICU. That night I put on the animated movie, Cars, stared at my baby taking in that she was still here with me. I made her comfortable and told her "I loved her more." I moved her just a little bit and she couldn't even speak to me because it took her too much energy, so she grunted. I told her I was sorry for disturbing her, that I was just trying to get her more situated. I went to my bed in her room and said to her, "You okay?"

She nodded "yes."

"Mommy is going night-night now, okay? If you need any-thing, you know how to push your button for the nurse."

She then nodded "yes" again.

"I love you, Baby Girl."

No answer.

"Irelynn, I love you, Baby."

No answer.

She was so exhausted that she couldn't even tell me she loved me. Early morning of that next day the worse three weeks of my life began. I was asleep in the room next to Irelynn be-cause she had so many things hooked up to her now. So I had my little bed set up, and I needed some good quiet sleep to carry me through. It was then that my mom came in crying: "Jennifer, get up, Irelynn's heart just stopped."

I ran out of the room, looked at her and lost control of my emotions. All I could see was the doctor pounding on Irelynn's chest really hard, trying to give motion to her lungs because her heart had stopped beating. I dropped to my knees, my face went numb, and my sobs had no end. I can't even explain the unimaginable pain running throughout my body. I was saying out loud: "No, no, no God, please no, don't take her, she is my world. I need her." Irelynn then came back to us. I went in to see her; she was so swollen and her skin was so stretched. I leaned over her and broke down. I could see an impression in her chest from the doctor doing compressions. It was more than she or I could bear. She was then put on ECMO (life support) for her breathing and dialysis for her kidneys.

Meeting Allison

When I met Allison DuBois, it was at one of her events, and I wasn't sure of what to expect from her. The following story chronicles the reading I had with her in February 2009, when she made contact with my little girl.

As I sat in the audience with my hand raised to volunteer for a reading, I worried that I may not be called upon with so many people having the same hope and intention that I had. As fate would have it, I was chosen to take the stage with Allison for an opportunity to hear from Irelynn. In the beginning of the reading Irelynn told Allison, "Mommy cried a lot."

Well, as I've shared with you, I did a great deal of crying. This piece of information coming from Irelynn brought me right back to the last time I saw her alive. And yes, I cried a lot.

"We have her on everything we can right now, Jennifer. I am informing you all that as a professional I have a feeling Irelynn will not make it longer than 12 hours, and we should probably just let her go."

So I processed what I had just been told: Irelynn may die by morning. Again, I went numb and cried for many hours and I found myself unable to eat or function, as a part of me was dying with my little girl.

Irelynn's grandfathers are her best friends. They have a wonderful bond. So I was aware that I was not the only one hurting losing Irelynn. My dad and I talked for a minute privately. We then leaned over Irelynn as she lay motionless.

"Hey Sweet Girl, this is so hard for Mommy, you know. Papa is here with me.

My dad whispered, "Hey Papa's Girl. Sweetie, Mommy has something very important to tell you." I lean over again, "Irelynn, we see you are struggling and so tired. Papa and I would like for you to know that if you want to let go, we are okay with that. We cannot keep you here if you need to go."

I then prayed, "God, I beg you, please give her the strength to make it to her 4th birthday". Miraculously, Irelynn made it. Irelynn is a fighter, I always said. But our time together would be short. The night before her birthday I had a feeling it was going to be her last night with me, so I asked the nurses if I could sleep next to her. It was a challenge because of all the lines, tubes, and just the idea of jostling her made me cringe. I went to bed at about 3:00 am on December 22nd. I had spent a lot of time talking to Irelynn about Heaven and all the good things I have heard about it, how much I love her and will miss her sweet face every day of my life when she is not with me, and how so proud I am of her.

It was 5:13 am when I looked at the clock. I woke up from a

very short sleep because what seemed like a bright light came on, yet nothing was different. Back to sleep. When I went to sleep that light came again, and I looked. I was in a dream state and I was seeing my grandfather and Irelynn. They had their backs to me and Irelynn was holding his finger. She then turns around and said to me, "Its okay Mommy, I get to go play now." I woke up instantly. "Did that really just happen?" I asked myself. Now its 5:46 am I glanced at the nurse; she had a troubled look on her face. I got weak then. I looked at Irelynn. She didn't look well at all. I fixated on Irelynn's vitals on the monitor and saw that she was fading right in front of me—I was beside myself. "Dad, it's time, she's fading fast. Irelynn's legs to her hips were black, her hands to her elbows were black, and her face was so cold.

"No this can't be!" My dad sounded so defeated. We cried together. We called everyone right away to come see Irelynn and be there for her last moments. I wanted to sing her "Happy Birthday." If you'd told me four years ago on the day she was born that in four years she would die on that day, I would have thought it the cruelest scenario one could imagine. As they prepared to take her off life support, my dad and I leaned over her and sang "Silent Night." Irelynn was in room 22. I played Christmas songs because Christmas was right around the corner. After we got done singing, no more than a minute later, that same song came on the radio. It was 7:26 am "Okay, its time, we are ready."

I was trying to be patient, but I couldn't wait any longer. I got on her bed and picked up Irelynn, cradling her in my arms. I stared at her baby face and kissed her as my heart broke into so many little pieces you could pass them through the eye of a needle. I put my hand on her chest so I could feel every last beat of her fragile angel heart. The nurse got a chair for me to sit in to rock her. I put my hand back on her chest. I kept telling her "Happy Birthday, Beautiful Girl. Remember Irelynn, "I love you more—and first!"

I felt her heart stop beating. I had just felt that last heart beat of my four-year-old princess. "God, help me."

The doctor came over, listened to her heart and said, "I'm sorry, Mom, she is gone now." He pronounced her at 7:45 am.

When I left the hospital I felt like I was abandoning her; I felt so empty, lost, and so heart-broken.

"I just left my daughter, Dad. I should be bringing her home like other parents. She is gone."

My dad spoke, "I know, I wish I could have taken her place. I would have taken every single bit of it. I wish I could take the pain you feel away from you, too, and bring your companion back." That was all that was said the rest of the day. I slept for days.

January 26th, 2010, my dad had called my sister in excitement. "Tiffany, I want you to call this number. See if you can get through. This lady's name is Allison Du...something. She is a medium/psychic on the JohnJay and Rich KISS-FM radio station in Arizona. If you get through, ask her about Irelynn. Tell her Papa misses her. Ask her if she misses me."

I was asleep, but that afternoon my dad told me all about him trying so hard to get through to the radio station. So that night I went to work, and went online to look Allison up. I knew nothing about Allison and the show *Medium* that is based on her

life. I went directly to the "conventions," and when they were taking place. I saw she had one the next night on the 28th, but it
was sold out, so I signed up to be on the waiting-list. I never got
a call. I thought hard about going to the show and really wanted
to talk to Irelynn. I went online and bought my plane ticket, hotel
room, and my ticket for Allison's event in Houston, Texas.

It was February 17th. I boarded the plane for Houston, I sat
down, and began to pray. I looked out my window and said,
"Well Irelynn, here we go on another plane ride. You love
planes, huh? I love you, Sweet Girl."

I arrived in Houston, and I hung out for a while anticipating
the event. It was about 15-minutes 'til it was time to go downstairs and see Allison. I again prayed. I grabbed Mr. B (Irelynn's
stuffed animal), put him in my purse, kissed my sweet girl's picture, and headed downstairs. I signed in and took a seat in the
front row far left side. Mark, Allison's manager, came in and announced Allison's arrival.

Mark explained that those who purchased "VIP" passes
could sit in the front rows and would have a chance to meet Allison personally. I remember walking up to Allison. "I really don't
know what to say, sorry."

She said to me, "It's okay, I am not going to pick you apart."

I got my badge signed by her and I sat down. I didn't really
know who she was or what she was about, so I really didn't
know what to say to her. I guess I was there for one reason, and
one reason only—to talk to my baby again.

At 7:00 pm the convention started. Allison filled the crowd
in on what she's about, what to expect, and all about the different readings she has done. I sat listening to her with such

amazement as I witnessed her doing these different readings. In the meantime, I am sitting saying to myself, "Irelynn, please come talk to Mommy. God, please let her talk to me."

Allison was specific that she was going to read murders first, and then it was going to be an open forum. I sat quietly in my chair waiting for my opportunity, if it came. I'm taken aback at what I am hearing from these other readings, so I raised my hand. Mark, Allison's manager, was on the other side of the room looking at raised hands. I was patient and sat there, still talking to Irelynn. Mark came over to me and said, "I am not sure what it is about you, but when I was sitting over there in my chair, I was feeling this really strong energy coming from you. So please, go join Allison on the stage."

I walked up to the chair, I sat down, and Allison said to me, "What is your name and the relation to the person you lost?"

"Jennifer, my daughter."

She started our session and Allison started to giggle.

"She is cute; she is hiding behind people, so I will come find her."

Allison asked me the age of my little girl. She knew she was pretty young. She informed the crowd as to why she asked this question.

"It is hard to connect with a child at a really young age because they are a little confused about what is going on sometimes."

I informed her that my daughter was four-years-old.

"She is making my lungs hurt. Did her chest hurt in the time surrounding her death?" I responded "Yes."

The doctor had worked on Irelynn's chest trying to resuscitate her when her heart stopped. He was trying to keep her lungs compressing, and this created a lot of trauma in Irelynn's chest, so this made sense.

I remember Allison snickering while talking to Irelynn. I could understand why I know Irelynn's a really funny kid.

Allison said, "She is saying something about McDonald's, or The Ronald McDonald House. She likes what you are doing for them, or with them. That is one of her favorite places."

After my daughter passed away, I started collecting soda tabs from cans to donate to the Ronald McDonald House of Phoenix. We're also trying to have a plaque made in her name. Irelynn is a very unique little girl. Her speech when she was two was at a four-year-old's level. She was such a great communicator.

"Your little girl says she picked me for your reading. So you were meant to be here. I don't know if it is because I have three daughters of my own, but she picked me for you."

That explains why I was there . . . me knowing so little about Allison and her gift.

"She says she really loves her birthday and birthday cake. She wants you to celebrate her birthday. She says it's a happy day."

I started crying really hard. Whenever it was someone's birthday, Irelynn's eyes would get really big and say, "It's my birthday, too, right Mommy? I get a birthday cake? I want a pink one. Please, Madam, Sir, may I have a birthday cake?"

Irelynn was so polite and very well mannered, but she was always confused about "Madam" and "Sir," so she would say both. So we would always let her make the cake for that person's birthday, and blow out the candles. I also crumbled because she passed away on her birthday. Allison looked at me and said, "I'm so sorry."

I could hear the crowd crying along with me, feeling for me. I was thinking to myself, "If all these people could have met my AMAZING little girl, they would definitely cherish every moment they have with their own kids and take nothing for granted. We had such a strong love for one another."

I remember reading in Allison's second book, *We Are Their Heaven*, about the unconditional love she has for her husband and girls that is so hard to explain. Well, I knew exactly what she meant. That is how my father, Irelynn's "Papa," feels about Irelynn and me. Allison then went on saying, "She is telling me something about her hands." I said to her that I touched her hands a lot when she was sick. "No, it's something you have of her hands, like a handprint/impression. She wants you to touch that because she is touching you back." Downstairs in my house I have a picture that I framed of her handprints, painted on a paper that she did when she was in the hospital for many months. Allison continued on, I listened intently and let her talk.

Allison continued, "She wants you to know that there is going to be a cure . . . sometime in your lifetime." She wants you to give her stuffed animals way. She likes them, but she wants other kids to play with them now. She has new ones."

I sat there crying and listening. I was absolutely speechless. I had her favorite stuffed animal with me.

"She says to tell you "Merry Christmas." She loves the gifts you got her, but don't worry, she was given a bunch there."

"She is telling me something about her face. She says her

face is better now."

I said to Allison, "My baby's face was really pale when she got sick."

"Well, she wants to you know it's better now." At the time I was a little confused by what she meant, and that is all I could think of. But when I got home, I realized that Irelynn had nine teeth pulled from the chemotherapy damaging them. That would, after all, make her face hurt.

The last message that was given to me really touched me: "She wants me to tell you that she loves you MORE."

I broke down. Since Irelynn was a newborn baby, I had told her, "Mommy loves you more, and I loved you first."

"No-o-o-o Mommy, I love you more, and first!"

Irelynn always had this cute look on her face every time she said it. I got up and Allison asked me if she could give me a hug. We hugged, I remember, for a while . . . probably something I really needed at that moment. I went to my chair, sat down, wiped my eyes and said to myself, "WOW! That reading was amazing to have Allison tell me so many precious things about my Irelynn that no one else but my family would know about. And I forgot to ask any questions. Crap!" I was so wowed that I never asked any questions; I sat there and just listened to what she had to say. There was more that she talked about, but these were the things that really stuck with me. That night I left the convention in such amazement. It also made me realize that she really isn't gone because she is always with me when she wants to be.

I now work at the Children's Hospital where my daughter received all of her treatment. I work in the lab and see all these cancer diagnoses and now say, "I can't wait for a cure. These poor children do not need this. Why them? The hurt that I know all these kids go through everyday they get chemo, bone marrow transplants, and spinal taps."

Irelynn has had over 70 blood and platelet transfusions and tolerated it much better than any adult probably could. Every time she received chemotherapy for that whole week she was so miserable, and just drained with no energy. But she never stopped giving, caring, nor loving those around her . . . something can be learned from the very young. As a single mother and a full-time night student at the time, I did take things out on her that I shouldn't have, and I regret it dearly.

I would always tell her, "Mommy is so sorry, Sweet Girl. I'm so stressed out sometimes and I never meant to take it out on you. Do you forgive me?"

I look back and Irelynn would say to me, "It's okay, Mommy, I'm here for you. I can help you. I love you." But as a mother, all you can do is treat them like any other child because you have such high hopes that they will pull through this and one day again become a happy child. But I have to say that battling all this my Irelynn had always smiled for anyone who looked her way. Irelynn is really well-known at Phoenix Children's Hospital for her beautiful eyes and for being a trooper. She would give her toy to any kid to play with, she would put her hand on her little cousin's back and help guide her to wherever she needed to go, and she would share anything she had. Sorry, I get a little carried away sometimes when I talk about her. She is so easy to talk about. I wish everyone could have met her. I always believed that when she got older she was going to volunteer, become a nurse, or become a doctor to help people—because that is what she loved to do.

It was such an honor to receive Allison's phone call on February 27th. I was having a tough day because it was my boyfriend's grandmother's funeral, and I was down in the dumps thinking about Irelynn and my dad, because he had been crying a lot lately. Allison asked me to write about my experience with her and a little, well a lot, and about my Irelynn Neveah. I got a little carried away talking about her, and I am sorry, but when my Irelynn passed away, I told myself that I would make sure people knew her in some way. And this is it! This was a brief introduction to the love of my life, my Irelynn. She will always live in my heart, and hopefully in yours, too.

Jennifer's Update

I thought this reading would be a perfect example to illustrate how a reading can keep on giving. Before I start a reading, I always preface with, "There will be some information that may not make sense at the time, but it will fall into place in time." A year after bringing Irelynn through her mother, Jennifer sent me these two e-mails:

So I remember in our reading with my daughter about a year ago in February with Irelynn, you were talking about a character that was purple like Barney. Well, Irelynn never watched "Barney," but I did figure out that I think it is Austin from the show "Backyardigans." He is purple and she loved watching them. And Austin is her favorite! Just wanted to share that with you!

One other thing, (sorry) Irelynn told you about the Ronald McDonald house and how she loved it. Well, it took us a year to get this done, but Irelynn's name will be on the walkway there, and on the inside she will have a plaque made saying: "All donations made in the honor of Irelynn," and it will be on the wall on the inside! They are not done yet, so I am waiting for the phone call to be there when they place it in the walkway!

My Comments

Jennifer had a long road with Irelynn full of ups and downs watching her daughter deteriorate from her illness as she tried to stay positive and hope for a miracle.

What the deceased comes through with I can always rely on it truly meaning something to them. It usually just takes us a little bit longer to figure out what they're trying to tell us, and sometimes it has yet to unfold!

Adam

Scott shares his story of losing his son, Adam, but in a far different way because in his son's case it was fairly fast and at his son's own hands. It's easy to empathize with both parents and sometimes painful to comprehend the reality of death. In both stories, neither Jennifer nor Scott had the power to stop either child from dying. Nobody did.

I meet a lot of various shades of personas in my line of work. Lucky me, traveling the world getting to shake so many hands and come to care about so many people. While touring the great state of Texas, I recall laying eyes on a man named

Scott. As soon as I saw him I could see his enormous pain. What I mean is that mediums feel levels of emotional intensity with every human being. Some people carry no pain because they have yet to be traumatized by life, and get to experience a carefree adventure for a time with any good fortune. They might make it through life with only the expected losses, such as loss of parents and grandparents. But not all people have that luxury; some feel great loss in ways that seem both unfair and unimaginable.

When I met Scott, in his eyes I saw a reflection of having seen things one could never really describe, because even if he did, it would still fall short of truly conveying that moment. His eyes also said that he wouldn't want to visit the pain on others by sharing the story at all.

Anyway, Scott "felt" to me like he was so full of intense feelings that they were hard for him to sort out. I KNEW he had to be read, or at least given the chance to be. Scott also had a very red coloring to his face, as if he was holding his breath or physically ready to implode. He was by himself and seemed not sure of what to expect from my event, that not being so unusual.

Two hours came and went and 15-20 readings later the event was over. I thanked my audience and descended from the stage and exited to a private holding room for me until the crowd dispersed. My manager, Mark, came in and I said, "Mark, you know that man that I pointed out in the beginning who needed to be read? Is he still here?"

Mark nodded in affirmation and added that he would go check and see if he'd left yet. Apparently, after the crowd cleared, Mark was walking back into the ballroom as Scott was just walking out. Mark walked through the door to my holding room with Scott, and I offered him a chair. I began relaying messages to Scott from his son. "He says you're not to blame. He says to tell you he loves you. You weren't just his dad, you were his best friend. He says if he could go back and un-do it, he would. He rides with you in the car and listens to the 'oldies' songs with you."

Mind you, my event was over already, and I was pretty beat, so I only read him for about 10-minutes, but when the deceased say exactly what is needed to be heard, the healing is deep and profound. I also explained to Scott that his son knew his story was personal and wanted it to be private for his dad, so he orchestrated this impromptu private reading. Just so you know, it's rare that I do a reading after an event because I'm so beat and so DONE. Scott's son did a really good job in being both persistent and forceful with me. He did it in a good way though; he just wasn't about to let me take my focus off his dad.

An hour or so later I saw Scott in the hotel restaurant, and his face didn't look red anymore. He looked kind of relieved and at peace. His color was normal. I smiled and shook my head as to say to Scott's son, "You did it kid, you brought him back to the living. Good job!"

Scott's Story

My brother was killed in an automobile accident in 1986 when he was sixteen-years-old, so I was familiar with the grieving process. Even so, that experience did not prepare me for what I saw on my patio that early June evening. My son Adam, at 21 years of age, was quite simply a good man with a big heart. He had always been a good boy growing up. After all of our experiences we shared together over the years, he had also become my best friend. I knew he'd been having trouble with his girlfriend, and could see that it bothered him. We went to dinner on a Thursday evening. Everything appeared normal and he assured me that he was fine. Still, I suggested we get together the next evening and hang out. That was less than 24-hours away. He agreed to that and started to get out of the car. He then stopped and turned in the seat. Reaching in his pocket, he took out his "lucky poker chip" from a Vegas casino. He said he wanted me to have it, that he had more. Adam reached out his hand, we hugged, shook hands, then he looked me in the eye and said, "I love you Dad." That was the last time I would hear his voice or see him alive. Sometimes, 24-hours is just too long.

I came home from work the next evening and heard the sound of ESPN on the TV. Knowing he was a sports fanatic, I was excited that Adam was home. I called his name, but did not get a reply. Walking towards the kitchen, I noticed some of Adam's clothing on a chair by the bar table and some of his things on the table. In particular, I noticed a family picture of Adam, his sister, his mother, and me. I just figured he was going to take those things to his place. I called his name again, but no answer. Thinking he must be in his bedroom, I went there to look for him. The room was empty, but I saw that his favorite picture of us fishing together had been placed on the bed next to a handwritten note.

The majority of suicide notes are vague at best. They rarely disclose a real reason or provide closure for the family. While this note was extremely troubling, it was not definitely a suicide note. I called his cell phone and left a message. I called his sister, but she had not seen him. I then called his mother, thinking that perhaps he was at her house. I read her the note and she became quite concerned also. As I was talking to Adam's mother, I headed back to the kitchen, hoping I'd find him somewhere in the house. The back wall of my living room is lined with windows. When I was about in the middle of the room, still talking to my ex-wife, I saw out of the corner of my eye a figure sitting on a chair on the patio. My heart leapt! It was dark out, so I couldn't be certain, but I was sure it must be Adam outside! By the time my next foot hit the carpet, I noticed that the person was slumped back in the chair, heat tilted to the side, and that there was a dark stain covering their chest, pants, and pooled around their feet. I was instantaneously engulfed in fear and my head felt like it would explode. As selfish as it sounds, I remember thinking, "Please let it be anyone but Adam!" Before my next foot hit the carpet, I recognized his features and, to my ex-wife on the phone, I began saying, "Oh no, it's Adam! We've lost our boy! We've lost our boy!" I won't describe the gruesome scene I saw on the patio, except to say that Adam, my son and best friend, chose to end his life by firing a handgun in his mouth. It's a sight that is indelibly burned into my psyche.

Surviving a suicide (continuing life as the relative of a suicide victim) is different from other forms of bereavement. It bears all the stages of the familiar grieving process, but adds other burdens on top. Guilt and the feeling that you're directly responsible for your loved one's death is unlike deaths from cancer or accidents. Society STILL attaches a stigma to suicide. My ex-wife's best friend abandoned her immediately. I was shunned by co-workers, and people assumed that drugs were involved or that I was a bad parent to let such a thing happen. Anger—if someone murders your child, you become angry, but when your child murders himself, a very confusing anger can result. Disconnection—my brother didn't choose to die. I knew that if he could, he would have remained with us. My own son chose to end his life, and trying to resolve that permanent decision with the love I was sure he felt for me was very difficult.

For me, the burden of intense, unrelenting guilt was the worst to bear. I attended a support group and found it helped to share with others who have been through the same experience. They did not judge or make the assumptions that so many others around me did. I read many books on suicide that were beneficial. The most beneficial book I read was Allison's *We Are Their Heaven*. Whereas other resources gave me intellectual understanding and told me that I was not alone in my struggle, *We Are Their Heaven* gave me real hope. Not just hope that I would someday heal and learn to get on with life, but hope that my boy was not really gone! That he is still here among us!!

Oh, how I wanted to contact my son. Yet, I was still heavily burdened with the guilt and disconnection that suicide leaves in its wake. I thought, "What if I did somehow mess up and I was the reason for Adam's decision? He chose to leave. That must mean he doesn't want to see me." As I continued to sink into the murky swamp of my own brewing, my thoughts evolved into a solid belief that my son was angry with me, hated me, and would want nothing to do with me—even if he could. I pushed away friends, hobbies, a girlfriend, and most forms of life's pleasures. While I felt I was progressing through the stages of

grieving, I was stuck with the guilt and disconnection. I was living a lonely, self-loathing life, and when I tried to connect with
my son, I was sure that I sensed only anger in return. How could
a man like me deserve to be happy when he had obviously
failed his son so?

I had never been to a reading. Frankly, I feared receiving
firm confirmation of what I dreaded most. I would visit Allison's
website now and then and receive her email newsletter. I began
to feel more and more impressed to check the dates of her
events. I was always "satisfied" to see there was nothing in my
state. "There . . . see, can't go. Silly idea anyway." Eventually, it
was bound to happen. Allison was having an event in a city
three hours from where I live. I kept putting it off, all the while
having it more and more brought into my mind. I finally said, "I'll
open Allison's book, and if it gives me any indication that I
should go, I will." (I gave this little chance of success, or I may
not have done it.) I stuck my thumb into the closed book and
opened it directly to the page where she wrote of the needs of
grieving dad's. I took that as a positive sign. I decided that I'd
been living in guilt, pain, and fear for nearly five years. If anything was worth a short weekend trip, this certainly was.

Arriving at the hotel, I was still very tentative. All I wanted
was to know whether or not my son loves me. I decided to grab
something to eat and sit out on the restaurant's patio. When I
walked onto the patio, the old song "Silly Love Songs" was playing. At the chorus, "I... Love... You..." Coincidence, I thought. I
was very nervous at the event. I still feared my son was angry
with me and didn't love me. At the meet-and-greet, I thanked Allison for her work and told her how much her book had meant to

me. It was a short conversation, and then I took my seat that I had selected in the back corner. I knew I wasn't guaranteed a reading and, in my self-loathing state, just assumed I would not have one. I finally had the courage to raise my hand at the very end. I wasn't chosen; I didn't know how to feel about that. When I was exiting the ballroom, Mark came running after me and said that Allison wanted to have a few words with me and would that be alright? I followed Mark backstage and sat down across from Allison.

I didn't know what to expect from a reading. I assumed it might be more vague, but I quickly became certain that Allison was communicating with my son. I won't get into all the details, but at one point I said I was afraid that Adam might be angry with me or hate me. The response was: HE LOVES ME! He wants to be with me, and travel with me, go on road trips with me, and he will even listen to the "oldies" music that I like! I broke down like a baby. With one reading, Allison broke the chains that had kept me in bondage for nearly five years! I literally felt as if I had been born again. I had positive energy and emotion swelling in me like tidal waves, forcing tears to my eyes for days. It was like being slingshot forward from total despair to instantly having a new lease on life. I loved everything: the trees were beautiful, the sky was beautiful, people were beautiful. Most of all, I felt my son and his love with me! I was like Scrooge on Christmas Day, after his reclamation. I didn't know whether to sing, dance, or stand on my head! The following day when I drove home, I learned that it is indeed possible to drive and dance at the same time!

The first night, I was afraid to go to sleep, fearing I'd awake my "same old self." I awoke about 6:00 in the morning, still feeling euphoric. I laid in bed for a while going over the previous evening's events and trying to get a grip with how happy I was. Every now and then, I had to get up and do a little dance to release some energy. At 6:40, the alarm clock went off. The previous occupant of the room must have left it set. It was on "Auto," so the radio came on rather than the alarm. The first thing I heard was "I... Love... You..."—the same song, at the same chorus, that I heard when I arrived at the hotel. I LOVE YOU TOO, SON!!!!!!

Kelly

I want to introduce you to Joni's daughter, Kelly. Like Scott's son, she was grown, but to both parents their children might as well be little, because to a parent our children are always the little buddy who wrapped their tiny arms around our neck and thought we were heroes. They are the babies who need us because we loved them first, and we are their home.

It is very rare that I do private in-person readings, because my schedule is dicey and can change at a moment's notice. I would feel terrible if someone got their hopes up to come see me and I was called away on business. Often my clients travel from far away, and that can be inconvenient for them as well, so I try and stick with my event readings and phone readings.

I cleared my schedule for September to do phone readings and be at home for the month, since I would be in Australia for much of December, away from our girls. My manager, Mark, asked what day, if any, I was willing to do in-person readings, and I told him on the 10th would be good. I go by feeling when picking dates; I let the deceased guide me and the dates they give me always end up being important to the person being read. Anyway, my schedule was set, and Joni and Ron were booked for an appointment with me. They had lost their daughter and it would be up to me to connect with her.

When I met Joni and Ron they seemed nervous, understandably so, but both seemed to be good-hearted, good-natured folks. As I began to scribble on my pad of paper, I felt "connected" to their daughter Kelly, and I began to write down what she was telling me, to convey what she was feeling. Without going into every detail of the reading, there were moments of humor and sadness, love and loss. Kelly talked about "watching the fireworks in July" with her little sister after her passing. Her little sister's birthday turned out to be July 3rd, and indeed this validated that Kelly was with her little sister on her birthday, right by her side.

Kelly said to tell her brother Jimmy NOT to get a tattoo for her, that she knew he loved her without it.

Joni shared that Jimmy was the only sibling that hadn't gotten a tattoo for her, and that three of Kelly's four brothers had indelibly memorialized her. Jimmy could rest easy that Kelly knew her name was written on his heart. Kelly kept pointing to her mom's hand and saying, "My ring."

So I asked, "Joni, are you wearing Kelly's ring?"

She held up her thumb that had a simple silver band on it and nodded her head "yes."

"Good. She says it carries her energy and it'll help you to feel connected to her."

I could see how much Joni and Ron loved their daughter

who had been diagnosed with melanoma at the age of thirty-three and tragically died within three months. I could feel how Kelly loved her parents and noticed how easily she came through due to her strong love and will. It didn't escape me that she was roughly the same age as my friend Domini, who had died of melanoma at 31, less than a year after being diagnosed.

Kelly said, Tell my mom that she was with her mom's grandma, they are together."

This meant a lot to Joni since her grandma had helped raise Kelly and they were extremely close. It was also one of the questions on her list. I explained to her that many times the deceased answers your question without you having to ask it out loud because they knew it was on your mind prior to the reading.

Kelly also asked me to acknowledge, "St. Patrick's Day, the birthday." Ron's dad was born on St. Patrick's Day. This was Kelly's way of letting Ron know that she was with his dad and he was okay. Ron was visibly moved by the mention of his dad being with Kelly.

This reading took place at my house, something I never do, but on this occasion the space I would usually book for the readings was full due to the Video Music Awards.

After the reading, I realized Joni and Ron were looking directly at my family portrait that hangs above my fireplace. Eye-to-eye with my little girls faces—how difficult that must have been. Existing after you lose a child, places you in an impossible spiral of loving to observe other people's mirror image of your baby as they are all around you, yet they serve as these reminders of the one whom you can no longer touch.

The whole Video Music Awards fiasco ended up being for a reason. First, it brought this couple into my house so Kelly managed to make it as personal as a reading can possibly get, as I was surrounded by pictures of my own little girls and family members. Second, Kelly worked for Sony Music, so "music" in essence is what she was. Also, "music" was responsible for bringing them to my house. I'm glad about that, so the Video Music Awards seemed symbolic of Kelly to me.

In the reading, Kelly kept talking about music being very important to her. Clearly, this is quite true. I also thought it was interesting that Joni told me that "Wind Beneath My Wings" was her and Kelly's song, because this is a song special to Domini and me. Beaches was a movie that Domini and I saw together, and I wrote about it in my book, Don't Kiss Them Good-Bye. How special that movie and song are to us. Coincidence? I think not.

So, I felt as if Joni and Ron sharing their daughter with me that day brought something special to me, and is a reminder to us all to never assume we'll grow old. Always tell your kids how much you love them. Kelly kept repeating in the reading that "she always knew she was loved; she always felt special."

Joni and Ron strengthened Kelly's spirit every time they made her feel loved and protected in life. They're the reason she was strong enough to stay "connected."

Ron's and Joni's Story

Our reading was scheduled on September 10, 2010. Our names are Ron and Joni Hewitt, and KELLY is our daughter's name. Kelly was diagnosed with Stage 4 melanoma on May 11,

2009. Three short months later, on August 10th, our beautiful daughter was gone. She died one week after her 34th birthday (August 3). In July of 2010, I was still grieving for Kelly and crying every day. I was devastated by her loss. We had been best friends and more like sisters than mother and daughter. If we weren't together, we spoke on the phone daily—several times each day. I just couldn't accept that she was gone. I had read Allison's book, *Don't Kiss Them Good-bye*, and then I read her book, *We Are Their Heaven*. As soon as I finished the second book, I went online to her website. I saw that she was going to be in our area for a seminar, and I purchased tickets. I also registered on her website and put my real phone number. This is something that I NEVER do, but as I was entering it, something (someone) just told me to put my real phone number down.

A couple of weeks later, I had a phone message from Allison's assistant, Mark, telling me that the event was being cancelled, and he asked how I would like to handle the refund. I couldn't believe he was calling. I knew something more was going on. I called him back and asked if Allison was doing private readings. He told me he would have to get back to me. From that moment on, we just seemed to be in sync. He called me a few days later and said it might be possible, and we talked some more. We spoke several times, making the arrangements and at one point, he told me he would be calling me the following week with a date for our reading! A few days later, as I was telling a friend about the possible reading, Mark called me right then with some information. The following week, on August 3 (Kelly's birthday), we were watching Kelly's DVD, and I said I needed to call Mark to see if they came up with a date yet. He told me that he had just hung up with Allison, 5-minutes earlier and YES, they had a date for our reading. It was to take place on September 10th. I didn't tell him the significance of the date, but I knew it was no coincidence. Our reading was also scheduled to take place two days after my birthday (September 8th). It just felt like the whole in-person reading was being orchestrated by someone else, someone who loves us.

My grandmother, Betty, raised me and my three siblings. I had Kelly when I was only 16-years-old, so my grandmother also helped me raise Kelly and, later, her brother, Jim. I couldn't have done it without her. We were all very close and even cared for Gram before her passing in 2002. As Kelly got into her twenties, she began to suffer a great deal with depression. During her most difficult times, it was Grandma that she prayed to for strength. She began finding dimes all the time, and I would tell her they were signs from Gram—she was letting her know that she was listening. When Kelly was dying and struggling to breathe those last two days, I whispered in her ear that it was okay to "let go, Grandma's waiting for you."

These things are significant because when we began our reading with Allison, one of the first things that came through was Kelly saying that we were more like sisters or best friends, rather than mother/daughter. I saw the perplexed look on Allison's face because she had no idea how old Kelly was—just that we had lost our daughter. I knew it was Kelly. She also said that this reading was my gift from her. It could have been for my birthday, but I think it was more than that. I believe that she knew how much pain I was still feeling. She knew that I needed to know that she was okay, that she had finally found happiness.

I would say this to her every day. One of the next things she said was that she was "16" again, she was in a good place and happy. That's what I needed to hear. She said, "that part of her never felt she belonged here on Earth."

Kelly had told me on more than one occasion that she wasn't going to live long enough to grow old. Then, Allison looked at me and said, "She's talking about your grandmother." I just nodded, and she said, "She is with her."

That had been one big question I wanted to ask Kelly, and now I know they really are together. She said that they love to sit around and eat bowls of candy and Fudgesicles together. This was so Kelly; she loved candy! Two of her favorites were Twizzlers and the Robin Eggs you could only get at Easter time. And, I could just picture Gram eating a Fudgesicle talking about how good it was.

Another huge validation was that Kelly was showing Allison her hands and mine, and telling her there was a similarity between them. I held my breath, waiting to see if Allison was going to mention a ring, and she did. Kelly wore two rings on her left hand for probably the last ten years of her life here. I have been wearing one of them since she passed—on my thumb, just as Kelly did. She said Kelly was showing her the ring.

Ron is not Kelly's biological father, but he has been her dad for the past twenty-one years. He loved her very much and was very good to her. Kelly's message to him was this: She showed Allison a coffee mug that said "#1 Dad" on it. She said that he has always been her daddy, and that he should never doubt what he was to her. This meant so much to him to hear this.

Besides Kelly's brother, Jim, she also had three stepbroth-

ers, Ronnie, Jeff and Kevin and a little sister, Anna. Her brothers
were all adults when Kelly passed, but her sister, Anna, was
only six. Kelly adored Anna. When she was struggling with depression, she would tell me that Anna was the only thing that
made her happy, and that she was the only reason she got out
of bed in the morning. When she was dying, she said that Anna
was the only reason she wanted to live. All of this came through
in our reading. The first thing she said about Anna was that "she
loved her very much and she could do no wrong."

Allison also said that Kelly was showing her the month of
July. Anna's birthday is July 3rd. Kelly said to "tell Anna that the
fireworks are for her."

Kelly also said that she had been with us on that day. We
knew this was true because we had taken Anna horseback riding on her birthday. When we got back into the car and started it
up, Ron looked down at the radio song display and it just said
"KELLY." Her name just sat there on the display for a full minute;
we knew that she was with us. She also said to tell Anna that
"she pinky swears she will never leave her." Anna makes me
pinky-promise her about something every day!

The last message she had for Anna was: "Thank you for
keeping me going and letting me see what life looked like when I
was facing death." This statement was so very meaningful to
me.

Kelly had several tattoos, including a beautiful portrait of
our grandmother on her left arm. When we started talking about
the rest of the family, Kelly said to tell her brother that a lot of
people were getting tattoos in her honor, but he didn't have to
get one. She said she knew that he loved her. Jim had planned

to get a tattoo that matched the "K" she had on her arm. Kevin must have been thinking the same thing, because he got it first. So, Jim decided not to get it. And it was true that several other people had gotten tattoos in her honor. Her brother Ronnie and her cousin Angie had both gotten one. Others were talking about it.

During our reading, Kelly said that she liked her cake. Her birthday had just passed the month before, and we had a small gathering in her honor. Our family and a few of her close friends came over and we had Kelly's favorite cake, Red Velvet. Her brother, Jim, had placed a lit candle in a piece for her, which we placed next to her photo.

Ron's father had also come through with Kelly, saying "Happy St. Patrick's Day." This was in fact his dad's birthday. He also told Ron he needed to get his heart checked. I keep telling Ron he needs to follow through on this. He says he had a complete physical a few months ago and his heart checked out fine. I'm working on him…

Kelly also said that she saw a male making a CD for her. The week after she passed, two of her brothers, Jim and Jeff, and a good friend spent hours putting together a DVD for her service. They all spent many hours picking out the right songs. We now know that this must have meant a lot to her. Kelly was also showing Allison someone holding her hand before she died, and she said they didn't want to let go. Her brother, Jim, had been sitting at her bedside, holding her hand, and he just snapped a picture of their hands with his cell phone. It is an amazing, beautiful photo, and they used it as the final picture in her DVD.

She also said that she makes a good screensaver. Just that day, Ron had put her photo as his screensaver on his BlackBerry, and two days before the reading, Jim had replaced a photo on my home computer with a picture of Kelly making a funny face. He told me he had changed it and that he just thought it was a really cute picture of her. And it was. She told Allison she liked her picture.

She had messages for all of her brothers and talked about how we don't have our BBQ's in the back yard like we used to. It's been awhile, but she wants us to start again, and for us not take them for granted. We will do this for her. She also said that she loves Christmas, especially the presents. It was so important to her to get everyone a nice present, never anything cheap! She said she will be with us and wants us to have a joyous Christmas, with no sadness. She said that she is the Angel on top of the tree.

Kelly also said that we will not lose any more kids, and that everyone is going to be okay. This is significant because our niece Angie, who grew up with Kelly and is just like one of our own children, was diagnosed with cancer just a few months after Kelly passed away. It was something really hard for all of us to grasp. We couldn't believe it was happening again. The outcome was much different, though. She had one tumor removed and she is now cancer-free. They said there is a slight possibility that it may return, so it was really good to hear this from Kelly.

Allison also said that Kelly had a white, fluffy cat with her and that we should ask the family who it belonged to. We found out. My sister June who lives back east called me a few days after the reading. I told her about the reading. She told me that when her cat had died she thought she had felt Kelly sitting on the bed next to her. I asked her what color her cat was and she said, "White with some brown, and long hair." I told her that her cat was with Kelly.

We are both so grateful for being able to have this reading with Allison. I do know that it was a great gift for all of us, and that it has helped me accept her absence with a little less pain, because I now know for sure that she is still around us. Kelly mentioned in our reading that I talk to her every day and that I am not crazy. I do talk to her every day and I have asked her if I am crazy. It's good to know that I'm not. She also said that I send her love every day and she sends it back. I will never stop missing her physically being here, and I will never stop missing our daily phone calls. But, at least now, I know for sure that she is happy and with Grandma again. Thank you, Allison . . . and thank you, Kelly.

Chapter 4

Living with Life
and
Dealing with Death

This chapter is dedicated to our friend Dr. Jim Hayes and his wife, Dot. He inspired the writing of this chapter when he opened my eyes by sharing his journey of dying with me. I've dealt with the grieving for years, but I haven't delved into walking with the dying and hearing in their own words how they cope with a death sentence. Jim was admired by all who knew him, and I hope by sharing his story that maybe he can teach you something, too.

Obviously, when a friend or family member finds out that someone they love is going to die, they're at a loss for words. What do you say to the person whom you love who's searching your eyes for the answer to: "Why me?"

They are waiting for you to tell them that this isn't real, that it's all been a big mistake. Nobody prepares us for death. We are barely prepared for life. That somehow feels more natural because we have some control over where we go in it.

Because of my gift, I've served in the trenches between life and death for as long as I can remember, and this gives me a unique perspective. When someone is diagnosed as terminal, they start thinking of all the occasions and special moments that they're going to miss when they pass on. Their life runs like a home movie in their mind, leaving them thinking, "This is it? This is how it ends? There has to be a way out of this nightmare!"

The terminally-ill start thinking of all the things they must somehow consolidate and "cram" into whatever time they have left with the ones they love. I remember when my friend Domini was dying of cancer, she shared that she really reveled in being a mom. She said it was the best thing she'd done in her whole life, and to please tell her kids of that fact. She wanted her friends to know that she regretted some things in her past that she'd change had she the chance to, and that meant a lot to me. She had shared this feeling with many of us at a party that we had in her honor a few months before she passed away. She was saying the things at that moment that she might not have said for twenty or thirty years because time was precious and it was running out. I wish I could have bought my friend some more time.

My own experience of losing people in my life to terminal illnesses coupled with counseling thousands of grieving people, helps me to make suggestions on soothing words to give to the dying that can help to give them some sort of peace, and equally powerful . . . what NOT to say to the dying.

When a person is sick, often people don't know what to say to them, or what to do to lift their spirits. Friends and family will have a mixed response to the news of the illness. Some will want to "fix" the situation by looking up alternative treatment methods, and I do encourage taking that approach. It can't hurt, and sometimes it can lengthen a life. Others will immediately start planning the funeral It seems to occupy their mind; it keeps them busy and they feel useful. We have a propensity to switch to autopilot when our mind can't deal with something so painful.

I think it's important for all of us to put ourselves in the shoes of the dying in order to begin to understand where their head is, and what we can do to ease some of their fear. When you're told you'll never see another Christmas, birthday or wedding anniversary, or that you won't see your children grow up or your grandchildren be born, it is mind-blowing. Can you imagine that? Being taken from the life you've grown to love and expect, from the people you cherish, an immediate overwhelming fright grips you because you think, "What will happen to them when you're not here? Will they be okay?"

I find the movie The Family Stone a great tool in learning to empathize with a person who finds himself or herself faced with a terminal illness, since Diane Keaton's character is faced with breast cancer. Put yourself in her shoes. If you want to practice stepping into the shoes of the dying, this can help you decide if you could shoulder being there for someone you love, so you're prepared when the day might come. The movie also makes you appreciate your family even more than you can imagine as you watch her focus on their needs.

If you were dying, you would most likely question God and if there is the Afterlife waiting for you, if your family and friends who preceded you in death will greet you with open arms, and how part of you is comforted by the thought of seeing them again. Shedding the body that's become the enemy seems like somewhat of a victory at some point, knowing that your spirit will live on. So many conflicting thoughts and emotions race through you, and the feeling that you just want to climb out of your body to be rid of the heavy burden that you just can't shake.

Now that you've put yourself in their shoes, let's talk about what NOT to say to someone who's terminal. One of the big no-no's is "Be strong, you have to be strong." No dying person wants the additional burden of having to worry about their pain "offending" others. If they need to fall apart, so be it! If they want to take a final life trip, support them. It's about them, not us, not what we need, not now. If there is ever a life stage when we can't handle others running an agenda, it's when we're dying. The ill want everything to slow down so they can stretch out every single minute they have left, and they certainly don't need to lose a single one of those minutes to petty nonsense. Each minute is so precious and fragile that each and every last one should be spent making a delicious memory and feeling each and every facet of life.

When a baby is born we celebrate them, this delicate stage of life. We cater to their every need because we love them. The same thing needs to happen when someone we love is dying; we have to love them enough to put them ahead of our agenda as they enter their final stage of life and they transit into the Afterlife. You want to make the transition as smooth and calm as possible for them with the assurance that you will stay connected, no matter what.

Don't start sentences with "You should...." Who are we to instruct them? Unless you've been in their shoes and died before, only then would you know, and I'm certain that's not the case. Telling them that everything will "go back to normal" after they die isn't very comforting. They want to know you'll be alright at the same time they want to know that they'll remain a part of you always, so convey that message thoughtfully.

They need to know they'll be remembered fondly and that you'll share their life with all of the younger generations, so they stay connected. Let them know your whole family will "expect a visit" from them regularly, so that everyone gets a turn to see how full of life they still are and also get a rather large hug.

Definitely don't ask the dying for a loan, because money for car repairs or your rent is the last thing that they need to worry about at such a delicate time. You'd be surprised at how many people do this not thinking about how insensitive this is.

Hopefully, a will has already been established and distributed in the family so there are no divides over material items. I myself experienced a divide in my family after my dad passed. It's no fun and it's unnecessary.

Try not to bring your everyday problems to the sick; they need to conserve their energy to fight their illness. The living need to lend our positive energy to the sick and be there when they need us—period.

I find it very helpful to suggest videotaping messages for people whom the dying love, so they can watch it on special days in the future. This allows them to be a part of days still to come. Letters are also great for birthdays for grandchildren or younger generations so they can stay connected and receive advice on how to get the most from life from the people who love them and have the answers to their life questions. Letters for wedding days to come are also invaluable, and such a meaningful surprise on emotional days. Letters can really be written for any occasion.

Music is incredibly healing and should be a part of a terminal person's daily life because it evokes good memories and lifts their spirits. When a person is dying, they reflect on every facet of their life, and often they will reach out to make amends. I always tell people to live life without regrets and as hard as forgiveness can be, it is freeing. Those who choose to carry venom and judge others will be their own worst enemy, and ultimately their own undoing. It's okay to be a strong person, but try not to wish others ill. It's not healthy for anyone, and the older you get the more hardened you will become. So, if there are some relationships in your life that left you bruised, do yourself a big favor and leave it in the past. Accept family members for who they are. It doesn't mean you have to like them. Instead of hoping that they see it your way, try and come to terms with simply having different points of view. Sometimes family members are like oil and water, and that's just life. It's easy to become stuck in our own emotional turmoil. Sometimes you just have to cut the strings that connect pain to you and choose to rise above it.

Immersed in Death

I travel the world doing media appearances, book signings, and VIP events. I work with smaller groups at my events so you're more likely to be read, and it's a little bit more intimate so that I can connect to my audience and they can connect with me. In one's lifetime we learn various lessons from a garden of unique people, and we can strive to leave the world in a better place than when we found it.

I've read thousands of people and I have learned something from each individual whom I come across. I try and write about a few of the souls who touch me so that my readers can place themselves in my position, and maybe even relate to me, realizing both how fortunate I am to possess my abilities and how, if I forget to come up for air in life, illness and death can take a great toll on me. If you deal with heavy topics in life, remember how necessary it is to have a place to retreat to when you're stressed, so that you can revitalize yourself. You're basically doing this to rid yourself of the trauma that you carry around from your everyday life, so that you can actually do some living when it counts. In my professional as well as in my personal life, I've observed some heart-wrenching struggles where I've seen people entirely change as a person as they attempt to move past the pain they've walked into.

People who lose MANY loved ones in their life in a traumatic way are often left wondering why they're still here. They continue to survive and "dodged the bullet" when the ones they love weren't so fortunate. They often have a traumatized look in their eyes, and you can feel the trauma literally permeating off of their skin. You'll see their guard go up high and thick. Grieving individuals often hold their breath and take very shallow breaths. They seem to almost be white-knuckling-it through life trying to avoid vulnerability, and they seem to become quite numb. I've found this can also apply to parents who feel they were "unable" to save their child. Parents and their children are indivisible, so the parents become the walking-wounded due to the trauma of losing their baby. The child died, therefore the parents become dead inside.

The other group of people that I notice carry quite large burdens are those who through their profession endure death daily, such as a doctor who has lost patients, crime scene clean up, hospice volunteers, firefighters, law enforcement, soldiers, morticians, or even a medium. If I left anyone out, I'm not excluding or minimizing any profession; I'm just short of paper. Many members of these kinds of professions learn to put the deceased first and fall apart later, or begin looking at the deaths as an element of the job, their life now, or both.

Obviously, at my events I'm immersed in some of the most traumatic deaths, which is why the living often seek me out. I sometimes have trouble sleeping because I replay the details of a savage crime scene or relive the last moments of someone's life over and over in my head, wondering if deaths could have been prevented.

I've seen times where the police respond to a call and arrive at the scene of the crime in time to see the flash of a gun through the window of the house taking the life of the innocent. A 30-second difference determined whether or not that victim would die that day.

I've seen devastating cases where the lady of the house answers the door with an ashen-colored face and tells a neighbor she's not feeling well that day. An hour later the family of four is found murdered. What if the neighbor had picked up on the fear in the face of the woman and called the police? Would the family be alive? I'm certainly not blaming the neighbor, of course; she no doubt would have helped if she could have. It's just one of those "what if" scenarios.

I occasionally obsess over the many variables involved in a crime. Sometimes when one variable is changed, the outcome can be dramatically better for the victim. I'm writing this because I am demonstrating for you some of the scenarios of trauma that we witness on TV or at work that one can carry with them through life. It takes a hold of you and becomes a part of you. This is so I can try to explain how to tone trauma energy down so it doesn't consume your life. I see people who absorb the tragedies on the news every night, and it wears on them. They begin to think the whole world is going to hell in a handbasket.

I remember watching TV and hearing a woman recount how her neighbors heard her being sexually assaulted in her apartment for hours and left for dead along with her small son, and they did nothing. Then the victim stopped a car asking the female driver for help, who then told the victim "she didn't want to be late for work." The driver took off leaving the victim standing in the road with her little boy in distress, and both in need of medical care. People who look the other way really destroy me. They almost facilitate the crime or condone it somehow through their actions or lack of actions. They re-victimize the wounded. I like to think there's a special place on the Otherside for people like that, or maybe someday a special karma will come their way.

When you're sickened at the thought of somebody not helping another in distress, that means you're a good person. That's a fine measure of one's soul, what your innate reaction to horrific circumstances would be in assisting another. I have to say, as you've read here, and I'm sure you've heard before, some people feel nothing for anyone but themselves—and that's tragic. When you see a killer on TV, they all have the same vacant look in their eyes. But for every non-human, there's 100,000 people who would have intervened on behalf of the victim, taken a bullet for a stranger. Hell! Cops do it every day! But it's the people who aren't expected to, who aren't trained to save, whom I want to call attention to. There are a lot of natural-born heroes walking our earth, and they'd never call themselves a "hero." That's what makes them so great!

God knows we need more people out there doing the right thing by others. Are you one of them?

I believe that there's more good than bad in this world. I believe that with every fiber of my being. It's so important for us as spiritual beings not to stand on the sidelines, but rather to get in the game and play it, otherwise another player on the field is vulnerable instead of protected.

There's a way to live a balanced existence with less fear, and an awareness realizing that maybe you're being too hard on yourself. For every one reading that I do where I don't connect with the living sitter, I have 100 outstanding readings that leave me feeling amazing inside. Should I concentrate on the rare occasion where I choose to cut the reading? No, and why would I? Why?

As human beings, we have gotten so good at beating ourselves up and become so self–deprecating that we automatically lose sight of the fact that nobody's a hundred percent in life, and we're not expected to be. Life is full of uncertainties and changing variables. Don't let others tell you that they have more than you, that you're unsuccessful because their car is more expensive than yours. They're usually the unhappy bully in a nice leased ride. They're often the people in the world who aren't the ones contributing anything other than their judgment anyway, so who cares? I have many celebrity friends who deal with being judged all the time. It takes a toll on them, and it just goes with being a public figure. The famous aren't always rich and the rich aren't always famous, so be happy with what you've got and not what you don't have in life, because someone would switch places with you in a second.

For the cynics out there who think mediums and psychics should be 100%, I'd like to talk to the people they've dated and see how the ex's would rate our cynics romantically, and see if they're rated to be 100% . . . most likely not. Were they 100% in school? Certainly not! Would their family say they could have done better in life or been more family-oriented? Probably so. Nobody is 100% in life, whether it's at work or in your personal life. Making mistakes is how we learn, and there are no guarantees, so relax and accept that it's the valleys in life that give us character.

Some of us will be born to have long lives and some short lives. Some of us are born to have our own children and some to love others' kids through mentoring. When I was a teenager I wondered why I didn't have blonde hair like Madonna. Now I'm happy to have my red hair. I was meant to be a redhead, not a blonde. We can't always see the big picture of why life's details have to be the way they are, but there's always a beautiful answer off in the distance.

I take the time to watch the wind blow passed the tree branches and through leaves like nature's high-speed traffic. I speak my mind even if what comes out of my mouth others would like to edit. I'm drawn to the dead and the dying when others are resistant to them. I'm a mother who gets headaches when her kids fight, but I take it in and recognize that I will miss it one day, miss their being small.

Prayer

My wise friend, Anne Gehman, once told me that prayer is talking to GOD, and meditation is listening to the response. I think a lot of people pray but forget to listen to the answer to their prayers, or fail to see that they received an answer at all. Learning requires observation and listening with your soul.

Let me give you an example to consider. I was lecturing and doing a reading at one of my events in Chicago. I normally open with a meet-and-greet and then on to the main event. At the end of my signing a young woman with a scarf around her head, who was clearly in pain, walked up to my signing table. I was picking up on her illness and her being challenged to live. After she walked away, I sat back in my chair to try and collect myself. I asked my assistant, Andrea, to ask her if she wanted to come up on stage with me and ask me any questions. I had never done this before, but I was pulled to offer it anyway. The young woman was with her mother and two sisters, and they clearly adored the one they felt slipping from them.

With her mother's help she came and sat next to me, and let me just say, there wasn't a dry eye in the house. It truly felt like we were all suspended in time trying to reach out to her with a spiritual safety net. I brought through her grandparents and she was quite happy about what they had to say and the specifics tied to them. Then she asked me this question, and I want you to think about it: "Am I going to live? Why do I have to die? I want to walk down the aisle and someday have babies..."

What do you say to that? Why her? Why now? These are all questions that we want to answer for her. What would you say to her if you sat in my chair? Think about it. The ill and dying are often overlooked because it hurts too much to have to face mortality. To even know what to say to the ill can be a challenge. They don't want to be looked at as a shred of the person they were when they were healthy. They still have their identity, their sense of humor; they are still in the game with us. After all, someone battling a disease could live for years and a healthy person could pass in a car accident tomorrow, so it's important to live shoulder-to-shoulder with everybody else. That's one of the reasons I write my books:to give the living the tools to hold the dying and reconnect with the deceased. Also, to reinforce the obvious, which is to live life extraordinarily large.

What did I say to the young woman? Well, I brought through her family members so she knew they were there for her, and then I conducted a mass prayer for her. When the event was over, she was bombarded by ALL of the people at my event hugging her, loving her, and pulling for her. She was smiling when I left. Positive energy can work miracles. That young woman changed many lives that night because the people at my event, me included, were paying attention to the lessons we were being taught by her life. We were listening to what the universe was telling us through her. A reminder that none of us have a guarantee that we get to grow old or that we get to be a parent or walk down the aisle. Take nothing for granted, nothing.

Pray, it works. It helps you to let go of bottled-up problems that bother you. It's good for you physically, mentally, and spiritually. Then meditate when you have some quiet time. I think you'll get more than just answers that will benefit you.

Get in tune with the good vibrations around you and embrace who you are. Whether you have "abilities" or not makes no difference. Try not to worry about everyone's opinion of you; in the end it doesn't matter. I've never fit in and I get it now. I wasn't suppose to, it was a part of the "grand plan." Even as a child, it was constantly pointed out how "different" I was. I have red hair. Strike one! I so obviously stood out from the crowd. I'm half-Hispanic and half-German. I filled in the "Hispanic" bubble and the "white" bubble on surveys. How could I choose half of me over the other? Strike two! Ooo-oo-ooh . . . and I talk to dead people. Strike three! I'm out of the normal club, immediately disqualified because of my unusual characteristics.

I recently moved to Los Angeles and found out there's an entire city of people who never "fit in!" It's the "land of misfit toys." How great is that? So for those of you out there who are "unique," congratulations on recognizing it, and get comfortable with it, because it's a part of you and one day you'll stumble upon people who totally get you.

I realized that owning my differences is so very empowering. A year ago I was sitting at a dinner table full of "Beverly Hills" women who were as self-righteous and judgmental as anyone I've seen in my life. Apparently my Michael Kors cardigan wasn't stylish enough to be in their presence. I mean, Michael is only a fashion designer and judge on Project Runway— what could he know about fashion?

They demanded that I "prove" my abilities right there at the

dinner table . . . not the most polite girls. They said, "How can
we believe you if you don't show us?"

I told them, "Well, I really don't care what you believe. I'm
not here for you. I'm here to visit with my friend, not to entertain
you."

I wasn't about to bring through their relatives for them, because a reading is a personal experience not to be taken lightly
or demanded. And I don't re-act well to people who feel entitled
to my gift and my time. I have it on good authority that these
gals are addicted to psychics. Well, happy hunting Ladies—it's
never gonna be me!

I'm taking my daddy's advice. I'm living life large and I
won't apologize for who I am, flaws and all. I'm not very good at
editing myself, but I'm super at living, and for those who feel like
you don't fit in, stop trying to. I swear being yourself and speaking your mind is like wearing the right size shoe, it's so much
more comfortable!

Teaching Kids to Cope with Loss

For kids who suffer loss, I find that it helps them to have a
shirt from the one they miss, mainly because it carries their
scent and energy. You can stuff it like a pillow and tie off the
ends with string or a ribbon, whatever you fancy. Kids can hold it
while they sleep, and it will allow them to feel closer to those
they love who are no longer there to hold. Often by holding on to
an object of the deceased at bedtime it opens a spiritual door for
a "visit" to take place while sleeping.

I sent my nephew a ceramic angel-shaped keepsake box. I
told him that if he wants to give his mom Deidre a message, he

can write it down and put it in the delicate container. I assured him that his mom would receive his messages. It's not that one must write the message down for it to be heard, but it gives the living a physical connection to the deceased. We need it, the deceased does not, but they still appreciate the sentiment. This gesture is especially helpful for children who lose someone; it gives them back some power, a bit of control in their young life. I also told my nephew that he could write down life wishes and place them in the angelic keepsake box so his mom knows what his needs are, so she can help him "make it happen."

Children are often the "unseen" wounded when someone dies, and it's important to help them to begin to move through the pain any way we can. Grown-ups need to remember to "take a knee" when dealing with someone smaller than them. Kids need to see you on their own terms and level. Children are natural "healers," but they don't always know how to help themselves, so it's our job to guide them and provide them the support system and the coping skills that they need.

I wanted to reach to the Otherside and pull Deidre back, but who doesn't feel that way when a loved one dies? Often loss makes us want to rip the roof off of Heaven and reclaim those we miss. It's unfortunately not how life and death work. We can however, reach them in other creative ways that draw us close in a different, yet profound way. I know children need to have their own grief recognized by others. and they also need to have a physical connection to their lost loved one So whether you stuff a T-shirt for a pillow for them to sleep with or give them a special picture in a frame, remember to do SOMETHING. It really is a lifeline for them.

I lost my dad, and I like to revisit the restaurants and places that he enjoyed in life. I know he's there and so do my girls. As a matter of fact, while writing this chapter I went to Buffalo, NY, for one of my events. On my last night there I had a seminar at the Hyatt in Buffalo. As I attempted to explain death to my audience, I shared with them that I take my girls for pizza because it reminds me of my dad. He always blotted his pizza with a napkin to get the grease off, and who knows, maybe it bought him some time. So our girls do the same thing; they blot their pizza and laugh, because the thought of Grandpa Mike puts a silly grin on their face and in their heart.

You can reconnect with deceased loved ones by going where they liked to go and acknowledging them when you're there. It's almost like placing a phone call to them, summoning them to be by your side.

So, after my event I sat out on the patio of the hotel. It was a perfect night, calm and serene. Joe was with me as well as my assistant Andrea. Our three girls were in the hotel room watching movies. A quirky man who calls himself "Ipod" was walking down the street singing, and he had a mesmerizing voice that bounced off the buildings and was very acoustic.

At the same time, out of nowhere another man walked up to me with a pizza box in each hand and asked if I wanted to buy one for $5.00, since the pizza parlor was closing up. I know I shouldn't have but "Heck, yeah!" came out of my mouth instead. A gorgeous, cheesy New York pizza was now in the palm of my hand, but not for long. It was on a one-way track to my stomach; I inhaled it. It was delicious and I couldn't wait to take some up to my girls. I knew my dad had sent it to us.

I had been meditating on that same patio on-and-off for a week, and never saw food pass me by, let alone present itself to me, so I was reveling in the circumstances surrounding me. Then Ipod started singing "The Circle of Life" from the Lion King, and he sounded just like the Elton John version. It blew us away. For those of you who read my first book, *Don't Kiss Them Good-Bye*, you know that's my dad's song to my oldest daughter Aurora, so she knows he's around her. Ipod had an extraordinary and relevant voice.

As though that wasn't enough for me to know my dad was with me, Ipod said, "Do you like Luther Vandross?" I shook my head in the affirmative as I took too big a bite of pizza, I'm sure puffing my cheeks up like a chipmunk. He then belts out "Dance With My Father," and I almost choked on my pizza. For those of you who've read my other books, you know that my dad was a professional ballroom dancer, so dancing was pivotal in his life. That song came out not long after he died, and is very significant to me. I was emotionally touched both by my dad and the range of Ipod's voice. Ipod then leaned down to my ear and whispered, "God works in mysterious ways . . . don't you think?"

In a daze, I walked back to our hotel room with the big, cheesy pizza and found myself quickly surrounded by my three girls grabbing at the pizza box. I smiled . . . we were loved. Watch for signs—they're right in front of your eyes.

The subject of signs is an interesting one, and it is far-reaching into our future because someone will always be there trying to get our attention. You never know when someone you pass on the street is living their last day, or when a friend you say good-bye to won't be back for another embrace.

Tips for Dealing with Loss

If you've lost somebody, first remember that they're not gone. Then write down your favorite memories of them in a journal, because the mind sometimes forgets important moments, and revisiting those moments later can be invaluable. Reconnect with them through the acceptance that they are there whenever you ask for them, and sometimes when you haven't. It's especially important for kids who've suffered loss to hear stories and positive memories around their loved one who's passed from those who knew them best and longest. It's our role as adults to fill in the blanks for these children by giving of our selves. This not only means sharing stories, but pictures and artifacts that are tied to the deceased and family history.

It helps to have something physical to cling to when you lose someone. Objects carry the energy of the owner, and we're able to identify the energy because we're familiar with our family's energy. If you hold the object and close your eyes, you can feel a warmth come over you and a strange calm which is your loved one putting their arm around you sharing the moment with you.

The death of a loved one can be a trying time, and one thing that frustrates me is that I sometimes see step-parents who feel entitled to keep their deceased spouse's things, valuing what they need above what the children need, and that's not right. Children are so in need of connection with those who created them, and that needs to be recognized. The step-parent's opinion of what the children "need" should be left up to the kids to decide, not be based on whether or not they like their step-children. (By that statement I mostly mean the sentimental items that pertain to the kids' childhood and family heirlooms.)

Another important point that I'd like to make is that every adult needs to have a will to protect their family as well as their earnings and the life they've worked so hard to build. When someone dies, the best and worst intentions surface within families. It's often explosive due to the intensity of the love that we feel for the people closest to us.

When someone dies, everyone scrambles to take a piece of the loved one's life that has ended. Objects carry energy, and they seem to draw us closer to our loved ones. Money is energy because work had to be done to make it, time has to be sacrificed to earn it, and money can make our lives easier when we have it. When someone dies, the entitlement from the living seems to surface. Relatives often break apart families fighting over STUFF. It's not worth it, and it's unbecoming to one's character.

I don't know if you've thought about it that way before, but it's what I see time and time again. An example of why the money energy becomes important to the grieving can be seen frequently in grown children who lose a parent. When someone inherits and they find themselves depressed missing their loved one, they are afforded the option to pay someone else to do what they don't have the energy to do. They can afford to go out to eat, hire a sitter to help with their kids etc., and this is a way that the grieving still feel taken care of by the deceased.

Fathers are often bread-winners and mothers often cook for us because they're born nurturers; both soothe us when we pain in various ways. Both of them take care of us in life and again in death. I think this is why there are so many misunderstandings in families as they tug-o-war over cars, bank accounts, and STUFF. It's important for everyone to try and be fair and considerate when faced with a situation like this, and not succumb to bad behavior.

Do what you know the deceased would want, and if the deceased didn't live life quite right and if you're in a position to right their wrongs with the living, then do so. The deceased don't hold grudges, so if the living say, "Well, she was mad at her daughter when she died, so she wouldn't want her to have anything," that's not true. People see their mistakes when they die, and making their loved one's lives easier—even if it's just a ring with no monetary value, but sentimental value—makes all the difference to a living loved one. So troublemakers need to step aside and let positive energy surround family and friends, not anger or self-entitlement.

Also, no living person should ever be making a judgment of another person as though the deceased is making that statement.. It's not healthy. For a positive example, you could say, "My son would want his daughter to have his ring. He wasn't close to her in life, but he'd want her to know she mattered to him"; but not a negative one like, "My son wasn't close to her, so he wouldn't want her invited to the funeral, and certainly would want her to have nothing!" Can you see the difference between the two statements? One is destructive and one is constructive. We all know people that would say either statement. I, for one, would rather be constructive at such a delicate time. A death isn't a green light for a family free-for-all to unleash every resentment over the last 50-years within the family. It's a time to remember what family should be and inspire us to live better, because you never know when the next funeral will be your own. How do you want to be remembered?

Often, grown children feel entitled to Mom and Dad's nest egg more so because their sibling was the favorite and had more time with Mom and Dad. So, there is often the temptation to take more than their fair share, thinking that they deserve it to replace the love that they felt they missed out on. I'm not saying it's right; I'm just trying to illustrate some of the thought process involved with loss.

Usually, the favored child doesn't care about the money as much because they had most of the attention from their parents, and walked through life feeling very loved. Many of these people have been my clients, so I've seen it first-hand. They are more concerned with contacting their beloved parent than just about anything else in the world. I'm honored to be able to energetic-ally re-connect them.

I'm not faulting either situation; I'm just sharing what I've observed professionally and personally. Some people get everything the deceased owns and still feel like they didn't get enough from them, because they are emotional bottomless pits. Others get a photograph that they adored of the deceased and are grateful for having been graced by them. I'm sure you can figure out why these two scenarios are so different and see clearly that it has NOTHING to do with the money.

I've noticed that when people lose someone, whether it is to death or change of heart, they tend to be "gun shy" of loving again. They develop abandonment issues and often push others around them away. This is understandable to anyone with a pulse. It's interesting though, as human beings when we're hurt it's a natural response to put our guard up to self-preserve, rather than to draw our other loved ones closer to us.

I experienced this when my dad died. A part of me died with him, so I became, as I saw myself, "unseen and untouchable" like my dad was in spirit. While I was mourning I was not always able to be there for our kids. I was depressed and I really don't know where the months went. I still have trouble remembering the year my dad died. After some of the pain subsided, I saw what I was doing: not being present for my girls. Now I'm there too much, reveling in every aspect of their lives. But don't be too hard on yourselves while in mourning; we're human and only capable of processing so much.

If you've experienced putting up your personal emotional fortress, remember this: LIFE doesn't stand for "Live In Fear Everyday." I encourage you to write down the word "life," and try and define what it means to you. Because, as we all know, LIFE means something different to everyone.

Processing Stress and Connecting with the Otherside

I, like most others, have a life that is full of challenges. Some are more difficult than others but all can take a physical toll on us. I write this as I sit on a plane to Buffalo, NY, surrounded by people who at one time or another have been wounded through the loss of a loved one, divorce, or personal failure as they see it. I am no exception. I've lost people whom I love, and I have had moments where my back's against the wall, just like we all have. It's a necessary part of this party called life, and it's really how we all learn how to persevere. It's the elements that contribute to making our days memorable that we all want and continue to desire, so it's vital to our well-being to pursue people and places that elevate us inside.

When I read people, I often have to remind them to BREATHE. I know it sounds strange, but as people go through trials and tribulations in life, and as we age, we seem to take shallow little breaths and white-knuckle-it through life. This is not healthy, and sometimes we need to be reminded to re-join the living.

As many of you know from my third book, *Secrets of the Monarch*, my getaway place is Pinetop, Arizona. I believe that everyone should have a place that gives them peace of mind when they're there, that feels like home. At least everybody needs a place like that. In case you haven't heard, stress will kill you! Even if it's a Sunday at the park, go somewhere to center yourself. If you haven't found a sanctuary, search one out. It will extend your life and provide you a lifetime of good memories. Our girls have been going up to Pinetop for many years now, and they love it almost as much as Joe and I do. It can be a multi-generational sanctuary Why not?

I also find chakra-infused candles in all sorts of vibrant colors very therapeutic after a long day of readings. Lavender in your bath or some epsom salts can be lifesavers after a stressful day. I find water incredibly healing, whether it's laps in a swimming pool, or taking a shower and visualizing your problems washing off you and going down the drain. These are some of the simple things that I do to soothe my soul.

While sitting with Joe talking about what renews me and keeps me going, I decided to write this chapter and do a little re-

search of my own. Bear with me, this is a first for me. I'm attempting to lead by example in unfamiliar territory. I went on a
mission to find methods to balance my stressful life through various activities. Some were more challenging than others, but it
was all done in the name of helping others to "let go" of their
daily baggage. I wanted to be creative, and most of us have
stress to release, don't we?

Joe has been trying to get me to play golf for years, and
the answer from me was always "NO." You see, when I was a
teenager my mom was very creative with grounding me, and
she'd take me to a golf putting course to practice while she and
my step-dad were at the driving range. Good one, Mom!

Don't get mad. I love you, Mom.

So I had always equated golf with punishment. I decided
that golf would be the best place for me to start. To tackle something from my past that was a negative and turn it into a positive
had to be a good place to start in order to balance the scales of
life!

I was up for the personal challenge to turn around a negative in my life and make it work for me. Let the games begin!

I must say, I severely underestimated the stamina and
strength that it requires to play this seemingly laid-back sport.
My body quickly let me know how out of shape I was. You can
be thin and still out of shape, trust that. I signed up for lessons
with Jack at our club. He and his wife, Sid, are worthy of a mention. They're first-rate people, and I like to acknowledge nice
people.

Anyway, I saw some of the women whom Jack had taught
to play golf, so I had hope that I wasn't beyond help. They were

40-years my senior, so my pride was on the line here. I purchased my own set of golf clubs and the cute golf clothes, etc. I
got the uniform down, now it was time to put those clubs to use.
I purchased a set of pink golf balls for breast cancer awareness,
knowing they would give me strength, too, through female ca-
maraderie as well as all the heroes the golf balls represented
who endured their battle with cancer.

My daughter, Sophia, who can fit in your pocket, picked up
my driver and decided she liked the big girl's driver better than
the kid's version. My driver was almost as tall as she was, which
made it even more adorable. What a sight it was to see her
swing it like it was nothing. I know it's SOMETHING, since I had
pulled many muscles in my hand with the same motion she so
effortlessly showcased for me.

Anyway, I signed up for a game called "Nine and Wine,"
which is nine holes of golf, and if you can stand at the end, drink
wine to deaden the pain in your body. We also have a game
called "Chicks with Sticks." So, I was grouped with Sid, her
daughter Marie, and Caroline. I was awful, and they didn't care.
We laughed, connected, and I sunk two balls. I'm told that was
good, but I'm pretty sure they were just being nice. Most importantly, I finished the course and conquered my past with golf.
Now it's a therapeutic outlet for me. You're with fun people, you
get to whack a ball as hard as you want, and find common
ground with other people who are trying to release some tension. I like it. I'm not good, but I'll learn.

My daughters all play, and one day maybe the grandkids.
Who knows? If you have a high stress job or just want a common hobby with your mate, take a lesson. If you are competitive

like me, you'll love it and hate it at the same time. It's a challenge. So golf gets a big thumbs-up from me! It's good exercise and it gives you an opportunity to connect with others in a light-hearted manner.

A lot of kids participate in a sport that, as they age, will fall by the wayside because they physically can't do it anymore, or their friends can't. Golf is a sport that can help a young person get a full scholarship to the university of their choice. It's a sport that they can do with their friends throughout their life. You can teach and play it with your kids, grandkids etc., and it lowers your stress level. What's not to like? There are public courses that are open to everyone, and you can rent your clubs there. So take a chance and try something new. If you already golf, then you know the benefits of it, too. I've also noticed that going back to nature has a way of calming your soul and soothing your nerves. By the way, golf really keeps you in shape; those ladies 40-years my senior still have amazing figures. Sign me up!

When you live in a big city you fall into the "concrete jungle" trap. Make sure you have plants and bright flowers around you to act as a sort of escape from reality. It's part of the reason that women get so thrilled to receive flowers; it elevates their soul to reconnect with the fragrance and the lively colors sitting before them. There's something about nurturing a living thing, whether it be a plant or a pet, that raises your spirits. I listen to country songs that talk about "watching the grass grow" with the one you love, and I couldn't imagine having the time to do that. I realized that it's not that they had the time, but they made the time, realizing what really matters in life.

I have my own version: I sit with Joe and watch the pine

trees sway, and we stare at the grey squirrels with their blown-up tails as they hop from branch-to-branch just above our patio. If you take the time to take inventory of your life and prioritize according to what is important in your life, you'll have nothing to regret. I've been guilty of getting caught up in the rat race that we all endure professionally, but my kids keep me in check in my personal life, thankfully.

I have two excellent friends named Amy and Traci who own some Massage Envy clinics in Arizona. They always look re-laxed and refreshed, so I thought checking out a massage would be a good method to find balance within me. Joe and I booked appointments together, and it couldn't have been on a better day. Anyone with kids will understand that kids not only can ride your nerves, they can instantly turn your hair grey. We love them; they're just challenging at times. The day of our appointments our girls were in rare form. We had gone shopping for back-to-school supplies, and the girls fought about every little thing. I thought that my head was going to explode.

We returned home and Joe and I left for our appointments. No, we ran to our appointments, hoping to extract our weary selves from girl-drama. My masseuse was a very nice lady named Jodi, who towered around six-feet-tall. I knew I needed someone who was strong, because I fly on planes a lot and sleep in many uncomfortable hotel beds when I'm on the road working. I found out the hard way that this is not great on the back and shoulders. I don't think people in general realize the toll that life in general takes on our bodies. I had many quarter-size knots in my back, and boy did she go to town on them! She explained to me that the burning sensation that I felt when she worked on my muscles was blood moving back into places it hadn't been in very a long time.

Stress and tension really do manifest physically, and it's important to love yourself enough to find ways to rid yourself of as many difficulties in your life as possible. I'm working on this, too, because it's very easy to get caught up in life trying to fix endless problems, and it's so necessary to take a step back. When my massage was over, I felt beyond relaxed. I felt like I was in a better version of my body, and I couldn't believe the difference it made.

I had gotten so used to the pain from daily wear-and-tear on my body, I just learned to live with it. I didn't realize it was making me cranky and tense. After the massage I didn't feel that way anymore. I felt relaxed, happy, renewed and a believer in the positive benefits of massage. It helps with your blood circulation, it helps your muscles stay flexible, and it takes down your stress level. I will definitely have to get a massage more often.

Needless to say, Joe and I left in a very good mood, laughing, and feeling sensational. I highly recommend massage as a health benefit. And hey, it worked for Frank Sinatra all those years he got a daily massage. He lived a long time and he looked incredible!

Joe tried "Hot Yoga" and he really liked the way it broke the toxins down in his body He did think it almost killed him, though. People we know love this form of relaxation, so if you're brave, it's just another form of exercise to help you to focus and connect with the energy around you.

Being relaxed and in a healthy state of mind is especially important when it comes to using your abilities. If you're distracted by kids and work or obsessing over your past, you're not going to get clear information. When I prepare for a reading, I always light a white candle and focus on the glow of the candle. I also do some deep-breathing exercises that help put me in a clear, focused frame of mind, and it elevates my energy to connect with spirit.

I find visualizing a bright light growing inside of me, and then extending outside of me, seems to act as a sort of beacon to the Otherside that I have strong, open energy waiting to connect with them. You can't be distracted, so you want to be in a quiet place while concentrating on connecting. If you want the opposite effect and you want to block the Otherside, then playing music can help you achieve that goal. Any amount of noise will shut down hearing the Otherside when you desire quiet.

To further open up, tell someone related to you who's on the Otherside to work with you on recognizing signs. This would involve them giving you signs to interpret for practice, beginning a clear relationship with the deceased to move forward on the same energetic page. It's like allowing them to hold your hand and plug into your energy, just as you've now plugged into theirs. You can also educate yourself by using pictures of the deceased as a tool to connect with the person in the picture. Often a physical image will conjure up a stronger sense within you, opening a door in your mind where you start feeling what their personality is, and begin to have pictures flash through your mind from that person's life experiences.

A photograph will also make the deceased feel a connection or "way in" to the person gazing at their image This puts you on the same energetic page as the deceased because both the deceased and the person holding their image are focused on each other in that moment. Write down any impressions you get while holding the photograph; it helps to bring focus when learning how to "read" people and energies.

Some mediums use objects that belonged to the deceased, and this practice is called "Psychometry." Sometimes objects that carry the energy of the deceased can make it easier to "dial in" to the entity that you wish to communicate with, due to the fact that it mattered to the deceased in both life and death. Usually, because the object connected them to somebody they love and was symbolic of their relationship, this can often be "felt" when you hold the artifact.

There are many various ways to strengthen the many facets of your abilities. Remember, they are limitless, and you are limitless when it comes to being strong enough to connect and predict. Continuing to practice is key, as well as being in the right head-space to receive clear, precise information through your senses. Whether you do Pilates, yoga, paint, play a musical instrument, or golf, whatever relaxes you will only make you better at performing strong enough to achieve 20/20 with your "third eye."

Chapter 5

Too Close to Home

I reflect back to Mother's Day 2008, and I couldn't have been happier. I sat in a dreamy room in the Phoenix Ritz-Carlton with my three babies (who aren't so little anymore), my husband Joe, my mom Tiena, my step-dad Doc, and my stylist at the time, Charles McCormack. Our girls were all dressed up with ribbons and curls looking like such little ladies. Hey, at least once a year we don't have to wipe some form of dirt off their faces. Mother's Day is that day!

We all consumed an alarming amount of finger sandwiches such as egg salad, cream cheese/cucumber, and chicken salad with currants. They were all a little girl's, or even a "big girl's" culinary fantasy for a tea party. It was my idea of a perfect Mother's Day afternoon.

I had six cups of soothing tea, but my girls had me beat; they love tea even more than I do. We toasted to all the mothers who were not there in body, but for sure in spirit. We talked about Charles' mom and my Grandma Jenee and my Great-Grandma Ruth, and we all visualized them there with us. My mom Tiena drank champagne, and she laughed and cried happy tears as she opened her presents. That day was one of those unforgettable days that never leaves your soul, and you spend a lifetime hoping for another day that's just as memorable . . . almost too good to be true. I know when magic has occurred and I am just grateful for special days like that.

It was a sunny day in Phoenix. I bet you have never heard that before. (Just kidding, sunshine is part of Arizona's charm.) Anyway, the piano music was intoxicating, like fingers tickling my soul making me feel "five" again. In my mom's eyes, I still am. It's kind of nice to be thought of like that and called "pumpkin" from time to time, especially when you're as old a soul as I am, but I don't like being called pet names in front of strangers. That's embarrassing!

Jeffrey Hattrick was our Tea Maitre d', singing "Wind Beneath My Wings" to his mother on his cell phone, as well as to all the guests in the tea-room. It's a tradition that he performs every Mother's Day. We thunderously applauded, and there wasn't a dry eye in the house. How proud his mom must be! We also enjoyed a fashion show. Joe is such a good sport tolerating all of our girly adventures. He is all-male though; he can be heard yelling at our television set every time his Alma Mater Ohio State plays a football game. He's really a great guy and such a phenomenal dad.

Anyway, the day ended and we all left saying, "We can't wait 'til next year!"

Three days would pass before I would hear the news that would change Mother's Day for my family. Joe and I packed our car up that Wednesday to take our girls to Los Angeles for *Medium's* Season 4 wrap party. As usual, our girls bickered back and forth for the sport of it. I never had a sister, but having three girls I've noticed that sisters will argue about the sky being blue or whose eyes are darker brown. It's tiring, and anyone who has kids or has been instrumental in raising them understands what I mean. I hear I'll miss the noise some day. I'll have to get back to you on that one.

Anyway, we checked into our hotel and cleaned up for a fantastic night of seeing old friends in Los Angeles. It was a decadent affair, and we reveled in the 80's music being played by the disc jockey. Our daughter Fallon hung out with her best buddy Maria Lark, who coincidentally plays Fallon or "Bridgette" on *Medium*. I think they drank one-too-many Shirley Temples. They had a blast together and later that night they begged to have a sleep-over. Of course, we agreed.

That night I had the pleasure of meeting Gene Kelly's son, Tim, and I knew my dad had to be there with me in spirit. My dad was a dancer, and he thought Gene Kelly and Fred Astaire were too cool for words, so he took me to see every movie of theirs that replayed at a local theater. The last one I remember seeing Gene in was Xanadu. This movie dates me, but being a former competitive roller skater, it was one of my favorite movies from the 80's.

Joe's cell rang and he pulled me aside, "Allison, there was an accident last Sunday." You know when you hear those words it's much more than just an accident.

"Okay, what kind of accident?"

"Your nephew, little Michael's mom was in a car accident and she's in the hospital hooked up to machines, but there's no brain activity."

I had just had my little nephew out four weeks earlier, and he was so happy. I know from grown kids that I've read that the day little Michael's mom was in the accident will be a frozen segment of time that will remain with him for the rest of his life. What made it worse was that Michael turned thirteen two days after Mother's Day. So unfair to a child, and so a part of what life can throw at you. Mother's Day and his birthday will feel heavy for him until possibly his own child is born someday in the month of May.

I've witnessed this play out in my house, watching my husband Joe miss his dad. Joe's dad's memorial was on Joe's 24th birthday. Our daughter, Aurora, came along two years later. Born the day before Joe's birthday, she lifted the gnawing pain from his heart that was tied to burying his dad. It's like those whom we love and are gone, send us someone new to love. Not that we miss our loved one's less; it just replaces some of the pain with the joy of a new life. And that joy is so powerful that it somehow balances out the unbearable agony.

What made it even more remarkable to Joe was that his "birthday baby" would see her first apparition around the age of 3, and it happened to be Joe's dad whom she described standing in her room wearing a "bow tie." Coincidence? Heck no.

The tragedy around my nephew rendered me helpless, and anyone who knows me understands that I'm not good with that. I prayed a lot, I cried a lot, and I said the words to my nephew that I hoped would act as some sort of buffer between him and losing his heart with his mother. Looking into the eyes of a child who experiences death so young feels like you're the very person who denied them their childhood; it's such a helpless feeling. I'm an empathetic person; I absorb people's sorrow. I willingly would help ease his if it's ever my place to do so. Time will tell.

I had some remarkable moments while Deidre was in her coma. I have been able to communicate with people who are on both sides of the veil, whether in a coma, Alzheimer's disease, or other suspended existences. Often the deceased or comatose patients communicate through songs as a way of trying to speak to us. They can manipulate energy because they are already partially separated from their body, and Deidre was no different. The song, "I Hope You Dance" by Leann Womack, kept playing in my head. I felt it was her way of telling her boys what she wants for them. I can't blame her, the song' s message is a lovely one. It's so important when someone you love suffers loss to not be the person who disappears out of their life, or to be the one who's afraid to reach out to them. They're free-falling for years, and need the grounding that only unconditional love can provide them.

Bill

People assume that because I'm a *medium* that death doesn't affect me, and that's not true. It's like saying that because someone's a doctor that illness won't affect their personal lives. Both professions have a greater understanding of life and death, but that doesn't make either immune to the pitfalls that await us.

Being a public figure, I do a lot of press. The upside of that is meeting the talent behind the microphones. I had the pleasure of being on a radio show in Phoenix many times called, "Beth and Bill in the Morning." They're a sarcastic, light-hearted pair. I met Bill in 2005 and ended up becoming friends with Bill Austin, and serendipitously we became neighbors. He lived three doors down from me. He used to stop over and sit on our back patio with us, and we'd make fun of one another and laugh until our sides hurt. One morning I was in the radio building for a radio interview with another station, and Joe and I ran into Bill. He didn't look like his effervescent self; he looked troubled.

Bill turned to us, "Hey, guys!"

We asked if something was wrong, since he looked so distracted.

He replied, "I got some bad news today. The doctor says I have cancer, and it doesn't look very good for me."

When you hear this kind of horrible news it's as if time stands still and the floor drops out from under you. It's so hard to fathom an end to your life because you've just figured out how to live. Of all the nice people in the world, Bill is the classiest clown one could know. He was a five-year-old trapped in a man's body, and I adore him. Shortly after running into Bill, the family and I moved to Los Angeles. I checked up on him from time to time. When I was in Phoenix, I would go into the radio building for interviews, and I always tried to pop my head in his studio and say "Hello," and give him a big squeeze.

December 2009, I had just finished my interview with "Johnjay and Rich" and I was in a hurry to get to my next appointment across town. As I went to exit the floor, a nagging feeling came over me. I almost felt pulled backward. I turned and walked towards Bill's door. I peeked in through the window and I opened the door to say, "Hey!" Bill was now a tall, beautiful, bald man due to chemo, but he was still grinning from ear-to-ear. You have to love that man! I said "Hi" to Beth, and then got a great bear hug from Bill. As I left and looked over my shoulder (stealing one last look at Bill), I got shivers up and down my spine. My smile vanished from my face and an ominous feeling came over me.

A few months later I asked Joe, "I wonder how Bill's doing?"

The next day we got a call from our friend, Pat, letting us know that Bill had just passed away. Of course, I was crushed. He was a light much needed in this world; he didn't have a mean bone in his body. He left his mark on Phoenix, and radio and television as a whole, for that matter! And he'll be remembered by my family forever. I don't know who tugged on me that December causing me to go back and see Bill one last time, but I'm thankful that I've lived long enough to listen to the guidance that I'm blessed with.

I shared this story for two reasons: one, to give my audience a glimpse into my life and tragedies so that you know I'm human, too. Second, so you never ignore that "nagging" pull that you get, because it only serves to help you. Ignoring it can create regret that can never be fully realized. I listened to my gut and I was able to hold that dear man one last time. If you EVER get the feeling that you should turn around, don't think about how it will inconvenience you or make you late. Know that angels have you by the shoulders. So don't fight them, because in the end—one way or another—you'll lose.

Joe

Joe and I had a door opened between us and his father through someone we had met. Please keep in mind that signs go both ways; they can send them to us, but WE can send them signs, too, acknowledging that we know they're beside us. Joe and I had moments where we sent signs to Joe's dad, Jim, so he knew that he was part of our special evening. We also shared a champagne toast with a new friend, Jim, whom we would eventually lose to the same disease Joe's dad had passed from.

As many of you know, my husband Joe's dad passed a long time ago when Joe was in his early twenties. He felt that after so much time, he had come to terms with his dad's passing.

I did a reading for a vivacious woman named Dot, whose husband was a doctor who had been diagnosed with pancreatic cancer. Yes, this is the same Jim and Dot from Chapter 2. This particular diagnosis is one that carries a very sobering effect, because it's not a type of cancer detected until it's often too late, so you don't hear of it being survived often.

A few months after Dot's reading, I received a call with a request attached to it. Dot's husband wanted to meet with me, but I don't usually meet with a person to talk about what happens when we die (meaning what they need to prepare for as they battle a terminal illness that can only bear one result). I made an exception for Dr. Hayes after my cousin, Mark, urged me to do so. Mark was in charge of my bookings, and he had talked to Dot's husband, whom he liked very much. Needless to say, I agreed to conduct the reading and I met with her husband, Jim.

Mark was right; he was a great guy!

It didn't escape me that this wonderful man had the same fatal diagnosis that Joe's father had, and that he also shared the same name, "Jim." The time that I spent with Jim was very precious, but what resulted from our meeting ended up affecting my husband in a very profound way . . . one that I had suspected was unavoidable.

After the reading, Jim and I had parted ways, and I walked away feeling I'd shared a special experience that would stay with me for a long time. Dot called me up and invited Joe and me to go to a pancreatic cancer fundraiser with them, and we accepted their invitation. With all the universal coincidences going on, I thought it might be good for Joe to be around other people who know what Joe and his dad both went through.

Joe looked so handsome in his tuxedo, and I was sporting some new high heels that I was in love with. (Ladies, you know what I'm saying about a great new pair of shoes!)

On the way to the event, Joe and I talked about his dad and our new friend, Jim, and how bad things shouldn't happen to good people, but they always seem to find a way.

Speaking of good people, Patrick Swayze's wife would be at the event, and so would Michael Landon's family. Both men the world loved and miss very much. I saw the irony in that Patrick Swayze had been in the movie Ghost, and Michael Landon starred in the television show *Highway to Heaven*, so they had both sampled an ethereal existence as actors.

We arrived at the hotel where the event was being held, and I took a deep breath knowing that it would be an intense night. It also happened to be Halloween weekend, so there were people walking around the hotel dressed like Romans, cowboys, and other funny characters. It was a little surreal, like walking into the lounge on Star Wars or something, an unfamiliar planet.

We met up with Jim and his family, and made our way over to the table. The night was every bit as emotional as we knew it would be. The emcee had everyone in the room who had pancreatic cancer stand up, so that we could see them. It was difficult to witness so many people in a fight for their lives, while trying to save future victims of this disease with their presence and fundraising efforts. They were all heroic in my eyes, and my heart broke at the thought that this might be the last October 30th that many of them will EVER have . . . the last anything and everything being played out for them, like the last song of the night. Nobody else would have known that Joe was struggling through the night, but I could tell. I know him so well. I ordered a bottle of champagne, and we toasted to our new friend Jim and Joe's dad, Jim, and their beautiful lives. We donated $614.00, since Joe was born on June 14th.

I know 6/14 must have been one of the best days in his dad's life. Besides, the number popped into my head, and as you know, I listen to the Otherside. I never dismiss the "powers that be." If you find yourself having a moment, and you want to make a loving gesture towards someone you miss, open your mind, and the gesture will become very clear to you. Joe realized that night that he hadn't processed all of the pain from losing his dad, and he became quite distant from me. Sometimes it's hard to understand when someone you love needs to push you away to process their pain, even when you really want to be there for them.

Joe sat and listened to speeches from other sons who had lost their fathers the same cruel way that he lost his. They were as powerless to save their dads' lives as Joe was powerless to stop his own father's illness from consuming him. I never met Joe's dad in life, but that night I felt like I understood my husband even better, and I love him more for it—and I didn't think that was possible. Joe wore a bow tie that night just like his dad always did, and I think he felt like his dad was in the room with him. Of course, he was. All of the ones whom we came to honor were.

I can talk to the dead, but I can't remove all of the suffering of the living. It's time to bring awareness and support to families dealing with this deadly disease, and maybe even help prevent someone in the future from succumbing to it.

For more information on detecting pancreatic cancer early on, go to www.pancan.org.

Family

I had to end this chapter with a woman whom I will miss until I see her again, my Grandma Jenee. She was very intuitive. She was different, unlike anyone I've ever met or will ever meet, for that matter. When I was little, she'd take me to the park to feed the ducks, and we'd bring Kentucky Fried Chicken in that eye-pleasing red-and-white-striped bucket, mashed potatoes—all that good stuff to eat—and we'd have a picnic. I remember her telling me to throw some chicken to the ducks, and me turning to her and saying, "Grandma, isn't that like cannibalism?"

She came back with, "Oh, the ducks won't mind!"

I still couldn't bring myself to do it, but I still laugh when I think back to that moment. Grandma had the best laugh, more like a cackle, really. It runs in our family, and frankly, it scares small children, but we can't help ourselves. When I was little, she used to take me to Dunkin' Donuts before skating practice so that I could get a Boston Crème and Coconut Crème donut for breakfast. My grandma made me a Muppet's bedroom ensemble when I was eight-years-old, complete with Miss Piggy and Kermit the Frog. I fondly remember the details of what she'd do to make me happy. She was a very tall woman with auburn hair and mischievous blue pools for eyes. I loved going to her house for the holidays. She always made me the best blueberry muffins. I'd go crazy for them and eat too many, giving myself a hateful tummy-ache. Unlike some people, she always got me exactly what I wanted for Christmas, so there was never a disappointment waiting for me under the tree.

Later in life I learned that my grandmother had Parkinson's disease. This was devastating to hear, because it was her worst fear that she would lose her sharp mind and quick wit. Grandma was moved into a care facility, because with Parkinson's you can have physical outbursts and require round-the-clock care. We took the kids to visit her regularly, and I'd bring her sweets and we'd sit and talk. Soon after, Joe and I had her over to our house for Thanksgiving dinner with our girls. We watched It's a Wonderful Life, and while the turkey cooked, I slid in next to my grandma and enjoyed the moment. I asked her if she wanted a Pomegranate Champagne Cocktail, and she replied with, "Do I like champagne, Allison?"

"Oh yeah, Grandma, you love it!"

We toasted to the occasion and I took a mental snapshot of the moment.

As I looked out the car window daydreaming about my grandmother, it hit me that I was driving back to Phoenix for her funeral. It had been almost three years to the day since she and I had shared the perfect Thanksgiving dinner together at my house.

My mother was devastated losing her mom. It doesn't matter how many years you have the luxury of having a living parent, it's hard to let go. My grandmother was buried on her 94th birthday. A couple of days after Grandma's funeral, we sat in a restaurant in Phoenix with my mom and Doc and had Thanksgiving dinner. It was hard; I had never in my life spent Thanksgiving in a restaurant, menu in hand. There wasn't much to talk about. It was very sad. We did, however, toast to Grandma's life, and we felt very blessed to all be together. I have no doubt in my soul that my grandmother was present for dinner that night, and she knows that the restaurant food wasn't even close to as good as what she would have made, because it wasn't made with love . . . her love.

Chapter 6

Readings

Readings are great both to give and receive, and although they can be heavy sometimes, they are amusing. Yes, I said "amusing." I'm writing this chapter so that you can see the lighter side of a reading.

I was on the phone giving a reading to a very lovely woman who was asking me to give messages and predictions for her children from the great beyond. I get this a lot, so I started writing the impressions that I was getting on her kids, and went down the line one-by-one conveying the information to her. When I got to her daughter's information and began telling her what I saw, she laughed and said, "Oh, I already know ALL about the trouble she's gotten into, I mean everything."

I was perplexed. "Excuse me?"

"Allison, as soon as I told her that I was having a reading with you today she panicked and told me every bad thing she's ever done. She was so afraid of getting busted by you and me getting mad."

She and I laughed so hard that I had to collect myself for a moment before continuing the reading. I'm glad that I could serve as a dose of truth serum between her and her daughter. Pretty funny!

Becky

I've given many, many readings and I've heard just about everything one can imagine. One particular reading stopped me in my tracks, and touched me very deeply. I was reading a woman named Katherine, and she wanted to make contact with her best friend, Becky, who had passed from cancer.

The reading went well and Katherine was very sweet. Then she shared with me that I had met Becky at my Tucson event a couple of years prior to the reading. At my events the VIP ticket-holders are given a badge to wear around their neck. Kind of like at rock concerts for backstage access, it looks like that. Katherine told me that when Becky's health declined and she was in hospice, she held the badge with my image in her hand every day until she died. I have never felt so humbled, as I was hearing that in some small way that I could bring a dying person comfort.

Wow! That really rocked my foundation. It also broke my heart that I couldn't do more for her. Sometimes we lose sight of how our actions affect other people's lives for better or worse. You never know, so make that extra effort to breathe humor and positive energy into people's lives, even if you're just opening a door for an old lady. There are lonely people out there who need to be acknowledged, and why shouldn't they be?

I was at the grocery store recently when an older lady knocked a bunch of gift cards off a rack. She was struggling to kneel to pick up the cards. I was surprised at how many people just walked past her, like she didn't exist. I walked over and helped her pick them up, and her face lit up seeing that someone cared. In turn, I felt really good because she radiated such lovely energy and had a really warm smile. So there it is, we took an accident and turned it into a nice moment. Life gets busy and seems to give us tunnel vision, so it's up to us individually to remember to care.

Many people carry guilt about not spending enough time with their loved ones when their loved one has a terminal illness. The living do the best they can, as they feel divided between their loved one's care and holding their household, their very life, together. Can you imagine the stress?

I did a reading for a lovely woman named Ame, and she was one of the caregivers whom I speak of who wish they could have done more. Below, she shares her account of the reading she had with me. She shares the depth of love that she has for her husband. Maybe some of you can relate to Ame. For those of you who haven't stood in her shoes, make sure you take nothing for granted, because life has a way of throwing a curve ball, and it's better to live life without regrets.

Ame and Her Husband

I knew immediately that Allison was able to bring Al through, because she was laughing. The reading was two days before my birthday, and Allison said he was down on one knee offering me flowers. She said that he was trying very hard to be romantic, and with a big chuckle, added that he was really bad at it. And he was, but that is what made life with him so interesting.

My husband died in 2007 from kidney cancer, eight months after diagnosis. He was 42 when he passed. The cancer was very aggressive, and nothing the doctors tried could slow it down, even a little. I was Al's primary caregiver, but I also had to work to support us and keep the insurance. I felt guilty because I couldn't be with him every moment.

After his death, I just wanted to know that he was okay, and that somehow he was still with us. I would get some signals from him: lights going on and off, doors opening and closing, and the dogs would bark at seemingly nothing. I even heard him talking a few times. It wasn't enough, because I thought I might just be crazy.

The opportunity came to have a reading with Allison. I knew Al would come through for her. He normally didn't believe in such things, but he heard Allison on the radio one day and was completely amazed by her ability. The day of the reading I was so giddy; I felt like I was going on a date. In the reading, the first thing Al said was that I was "Florence Nightingale," and that I had been his caretaker and had been so nurturing. He expressed his gratitude and needed me to know that he was no longer feeling any pain. Allison described his passing just as it happened. He just slipped away after sleeping for several days.

During the reading, Allison spoke of many aspects of our life together, and the details were amazing. She was so accurate, but that wasn't what captivated me. This was really Al with us. She brought him through... his personality, his sense of humor, his excitement for life. These weren't just details being revealed to me; it was my husband. He advised me that I should take dancing lessons. It's something he wanted to do with me, but never got the chance. He said he really needed it. He laughed and told Allison that he had his own moves, but not really what the ladies like. We were all laughing, and I could just picture the silly grin he gave Allison when he said it. When the reading was over, Allison said that she was leaving Al with me.

That night, I was watching television. I felt a sensation on my leg as if someone was rubbing it. I knew it was Al. Since the reading, I have felt lighter. The guilt I had has lifted. I gave him the best care that I could, and he appreciated it. I now know that he is okay and that I will see him again. Not surprisingly, Allison had said that he was in a good place energetically and had a very strong soul. In life, he lived life with passion and cared deeply for those he loved. I'm not surprised that he would have the same energy in death. I am very grateful to Allison for the opportunity to speak with my husband. I still miss him, but I know that he is okay and that he is still with me.

Australia

I toured Australia, a country that I love, because the people are so centered and upbeat. I had some interesting readings. Here are some of the lighter moments that occurred:

A family showed up that had lost their husband/dad recently. During the reading, "man of the hour" said, "Tell my family my shoes aren't that great! They don't have to keep them."

The wife gasped and the son looked at her in awe. They then told me that the son was wearing his dad's shoes right now, special for the event, in hopes he'd recognize the gesture.

Well, he did.

I read some grown daughters who'd lost their mum, and

they were struggling with the loss. The information was coming through easy, yet somber. Then the deceased said, "Tell my girls to not forget what I cooked for them, to show them I loved them. And they should make some of those same dishes for their kids. They always told me how good it was."

The daughters started laughing, like they just heard the best comedy line ever.

They said, "We always told Mum how good her cooking was to not hurt her feelings. She was a terrible cook. She burnt most things she tried to make."

I followed with, "Well, she knows now!"

They chuckled again, and they all left with smiles on their faces. What a satisfying moment.

Sean

My son, Sean, lived with his grandmother and was doing very well. Sean was working for UPS part-time, and planned to go to school to become a manager for UPS.

On May 17, 2010, I received a call that no parent wants to receive . . . that is to hear that your child has been in a bad car accident, and it doesn't look good.

My sister, Penny, kept on telling me that Sean wasn't doing well, and she was going to head to the hospital to see what was going on. It was 1:30 in the morning Texas-time and 12:30 am Georgia-time. It took me all day to get plane tickets to get me to my son, so that I could be by his side. Ryan, my oldest son, came with me, and we arrived in Texas around 9 pm that night. It felt like an eternity to get there. My husband, Ron, and Casey, Sean's younger brother, would arrive the next day.

As I walked into the emergency room, I just couldn't believe that my son had been in a car accident, and that he might not make it through the night. Ryan and I walked in the back room and we saw Sean. He looked at peace. For someone just having had a car accident, he didn't have any major cuts, except on his chin—but his arm and his neck were broken. The nurse told me, "You can touch him." And when I did, I knew he wasn't with me any longer. I didn't sense he was in his body.

My husband Ron and son Casey arrived, and the whole family stood by Sean's bed, including all of his friends. We prayed to GOD to watch our son and give him peace.

We at that point decided that if Sean couldn't come back to us, and his organs were still good, that Sean would want to be an organ donor and give life to others. And that's exactly what he did.

When I came back from Dallas, I went back to work right away, but I felt like there was something pushing me to go to the book store and look at books that would give me strength in the Afterlife. So, I followed the need to go, and while I was there I saw Allison's book, *We are Their Heaven*, and I bought it.

This is important because with my 2nd reading, Sean had told me that he gave me her book. This also explained why I felt like I was being prodded to buy her book. When I saw it, I felt his energy so strongly.

On March 13th, I met Allison at one of her events, and I told my sister that Sean is "definitely here," and he was.

That night, I was one of the audience members who received a reading, and Sean came through. He sounded so happy! He told Allison that he was in a good place and that he liked the necklace that his brother wore. The necklace had a guitar on it, and read "RIP Sean." He said that he liked the picture in the living room of him. The picture is big and it is Sean sitting in front of a motorcycle and smiling. I was so relieved after the reading. But I wanted more.

I had my 2nd reading with Allison over the phone on April 6th, 2011.

Allison stated that she would "bring him through," and that it might take a few seconds. There was silence on the phone, but then she jumped right into the reading. Allison asked how long Sean had been gone, and I said it had been 11 months. Allison stated, "It is very rare to have a person who has been gone for such a short time to come through so strong." She also said that Sean and I had a very strong energy binding us together.

Allison started laughing because Sean kept saying he was the "good-looking one." Sean was taller than his older brother Ryan, and Ryan never liked being short. And Sean had blue eyes and blond hair. He was a great-looking young man. Sean had even said that he could have been an actor or model, and it's very true.

Sean's personality was very strong. He was the jokester amongst his friends; he could always make someone roar with laughter. Many of his friends said that the party didn't really start until Sean walked into the room. This is important because in the reading Sean said that no one could believe that Sean was gone because he was the "golden boy."

Allison also said that she sees a domino effect with Sean's friends, that his death has changed them all. And I do know that, because of Sean passing away, that many of them have stopped drinking, and they started turning their life around for the better.

Allison asked me if I had any questions so far, and I asked her to ask Sean what happened the night of the accident. And he said that he wasn't paying attention when he was driving, and he tried to get out of the accident, but he couldn't fix it. He had always landed on his feet throughout his life, but was unable to correct this. Sean thought he was invincible, and he wasn't. This was one time when even I couldn't get him out of a bad situation. This is important because I was always with Sean when he got in trouble, and never left his side. It would always turn out okay, but this time it didn't.

Sean wanted me to know that I couldn't have prevented his passing. He wanted me to know that it was his time, and there was nothing I could do.

Sean explained that he was now like a counselor helping children cross over, and that children like him. Children did like Sean, but he would always tease them and run after them. He was a big kid.

Sean said that his cell phone is very important because he plays with it still, and it carries his energy.

His brother Casey has his cell phone. Casey wouldn't let me change Sean's number. After the reading, I asked Casey about Sean's phone, and he said, "Yes," he thought that something was wrong with his phone because there have been three times that Casey has gotten a missed call from Sean.

I said, "No, it's not broken; its Sean's energy."

In the reading, when Allison told me about the missed calls, it was so nice to know that Sean was telling us that he was okay and still reaching out.

Sean said that he still leaves the refrigerator door open. And there are mornings when I wake up and the refrigerator door is open. That's my boy!

Before I could ask Allison whom he was with, Sean explained that he was "with my dad."

Sean was always very close to his granddad, so that didn't surprise me. Also, in the reading my dad said that he was sorry for the pain he had caused me, and that he was very proud of me and that he loved me. My father died at the age of 57. He was very young, and I always felt guilty because I didn't get to say good-bye.

Sean said he was with a man who had a lot of cancer. That was my grandfather who was a Baptist preacher. My grandfather said I raised a good son.

The last time my grandfather saw Sean was when he was 4 or 5-years-old, so it was comforting to know they were together.

Allison said, "Sean is with your grandmother on your mother's side."

I started crying because my youngest sister, Rebecka, had a dream the week before my reading and my grandmother and Sean were together. They were very happy. My youngest sister was so happy to see them in the dream, and they all exchanged hugs and kisses. She said she didn't want it to end. In the dream, Sean and my grandmother told my sister to go because they were happy and fine.

Sean also said for me not to worry because the women on my mother's side of the family love to cook, so he is eating and well taken care of. It makes me feel better knowing that they are taking care of my Sean.

The older generations on my dad's side and my mom's side loved to bake and cook, so when Sean told me that he was being taken care of, I was so happy that all my grandparents were with Sean.

Sean also talked about a picture where he was being a clown, and making funny faces and rabbit ears behind a male's head. This picture was taken the week that my oldest son graduated. Sean insisted that he was "still in the family," and we know that he will always remain with us.

Sean kept showing Allison a black cat that he was playfully teasing that he said he now took care of. I checked on this, and it was his girlfriend's cat. He also said that his girlfriend will never really get over him, but he really wants her to be happy again.

When I asked Allison about Sean's older brother, Sean said he was worried because Ryan keeps staring at the computer, and he is very depressed. He looks at pictures of him and listens to music they both liked.

Sean and Ryan were very close; they did everything together. Ryan really doesn't know how to go on without Sean. But Sean said, "We can still hang out together, Bro!"

I have had many dreams about Sean, and they are all when he is around the age of 6. In the reading, Sean stated that he doesn't look 6-years-old in Heaven, he's older. But that "being little" was his best time, because he was able to be my little man. He wanted me to take a picture out of him at that age, and remember he'll always be my little boy.

He also said that there is a picture of him holding a bat. It was Sean's baseball picture, and he later decided that he hated baseball, so I think he was trying to be funny.

Allison said that April is very important to Sean, meaning that there is a passing or a birthday in April to somebody close to Sean.

My birthday is in April, and so is my sister's, Rebecka. Sean also said he wants me to hide Easter eggs, and he wants an Easter basket. There wasn't a year that would pass where I didn't surprise my sons with Easter baskets, no matter how old they got.

Sean and his father were very close, but after Sean passed away, Ron, his father, had a very hard time with losing Sean. Sean said to tell Dad that he was "the best," and that he let him get away with everything! And that there is a picture of Sean, Ryan, and Ron when Sean was knee-high of Ron, and Ron had his arms around both of them. Sean said he felt very loved and stated that Ron showed a lot of affection to his boys that he never would show to anyone else. Sean always said that his dad was very smart; he knew a little about everything. And in the reading, he reiterated that sentiment.

Sean often downloaded a lot of music, and he said that his friends are now downloading his music. He also said he loved his Guitar Hero, and he wanted his brother to have it. Sean would always play that game with Casey; he loved their time together playing Guitar Hero.

Sean also pointed out that there is a picture of me kneeling down, and I'm giving him a hug, and he said it is the age I see him being in my dreams. I remember that picture, and it is my

Sean.

Sean loved music, and in the reading he was playing "Love Me Tender" from Elvis Presley. I remember my mother telling me that my dad and she would listen to "Love Me Tender." I think this was Sean's way of acknowledging that my dad was there with him.

Also, when I bought Sean his first guitar, he taught himself how to play "Stairway to Heaven," which happened to be my favorite song, and in the reading Allison told me that Sean was playing "Stairway to Heaven."

When Sean passed away in May, it was very hard. He was only 21 years of age. On September 2nd, he would have turned 22, and we blew up balloons and put notes inside of them. He said in the reading that he got them. He also said that he didn't like flowers, but instead to send him red balloons. He loves the color red.

In the reading, he said that he likes American muscle cars. Sean kept showing Allison a red car, in particular. Sean had a red Camero. It was the car he was driving when he had his fatal accident. Allison said that in his Heaven, the car is fine and he's still driving it. Sean loved his car.

Sean also said that he was sorry that he ruined Mother's Day, but that the date of the 17th was very meaningful. The 17th was the day that Sean passed away. Sean kept pointing out the time he said that they "got the time wrong."

I truly believe this, because I received a text at 3:20 am that said, "I love you, Mom." That is when Sean died—not at 12:17 pm.

The readings have changed my life. I feel strength and

comfort and I am not afraid to die, although I was informed by Allison that I will live a long life. I will live my life to the fullest, knowing that my son is with still with me.

Sean was and still is my strength. We were very close, and I still feel the energy that we both have together. Sean pushed me to go to Allison Dubois' event and to pick up her book. He did this so that I would find some level of peace. I know that I will have my hard days, and there will be days that I will feel like nothing ever happened.

I know Sean wants me to be happy, and I will go on with his strength.

Like Sean said during the reading, "Mom, remember what you always told me? One day at a time."

My experience with Sean

Sean came through extremely effortlessly, even before the reading someone kept whispering "son" in my ear. I didn't share that with his mom, Debra, but now she knows.

Sean told me he was "so impatient." In other words, he was very ready to talk to his mom. And that's where I come in.

Sean's energy was comical, yet cool and loving. He had a really big heart, still does. He came through confident, yet concerned about his family. He kept referencing "muscle cars," and he kept flashing the image of a red car through my head. It turns out that Sean was in a red Camero when he was in the car accident.

Sean talked about his cell phone and how he tries to communicate through it. He still plays with it so his family knows he's there. Debra confirmed that Sean's brother has his cell phone, and has experienced some strange activity through it since Sean's passing.

Sean repeatedly flashed the number "17" through my head, so I told Debra, and she shared with me that Sean had died on the 17th of May. It was the only number that he shared with me during his reading.

Sean wrote the word "April" in my mind, and this usually means there was a birthday or a passing in that month connected to someone the deceased loves. Debra shared that her birthday is in April, as well as her sister's, so that's Sean's way of saying he'll be at the celebrations.

During the reading, Sean shared many personal details about his life and his family, and it was mesmerizing seeing Sean lift his mother's spirit to a place that it hadn't been in a very long time. I liked that Sean said, "Tell my mom I still leave the refrigerator door open while I figure out what I want to eat!"

Debra laughed and said that she wakes up some mornings and the refrigerator door is open, and now she knows why. I really like that we take our sense of humor with us.

He talked about having the best parents in the world, and loving his brothers. He spoke of specific family members whom he's around now, and still being a member of his living family. Sean played "Stairway to Heaven" in my head, and I shared this with Debra. It's one of her favorite songs, so this touched her. I'm fond of Sean and Debra. They're good people, the kind of people our world needs more of. So, as you read this, send good thoughts to them both, and remember them. Debra's hoping that by letting us be a part of her journey that maybe it will help another family who can relate, so they know that those we love never leave us.

Sean was an organ donor, and through his death he saved many lives . . . something to consider when you make a living will or get a driver's license. I'm an organ donor. I know that when you die you become whole again in spirit, so there's nothing to miss.

Debra knows that our heartstrings keep us connected to our babies and those we love more than life itself.

Sean is still in his family portrait, and he will continue forward with them throughout their life, until they meet again.

That's Rich!

I did a reading for one of my very good friends who left a lasting impression on me, because it was so personal. I mean if I read him, I wanted it to be really great, but I had no doubt that Rich's mom would come through. I didn't actually read Rich until 3 years after we met and became friends. I waited because the timing had to be right, and it hadn't felt quite strong enough before. As soon as I got that urgent feeling that I get when the Otherside prods me to read someone close to me, I know the time has finally come. Honestly, I don't like to read people close to me because it redefines the relationship, so I usually keep my friendships separate from my work. Often mixing business with friends causes social events to also become work. Rich is an exception, though, he's not like that; he never oversteps my boundaries. As a matter of fact, I was kind of excited that the time had come. After all, I got to meet one of my good friend's mother, a woman who had met few new living people since she had died almost twenty years ago.

When Rich's sandy blonde hair and wide smile came bounding through my front door, I immediately ushered him into my office. Rich is a man who never runs out of things to say or music trivia to challenge you with, and he uses humor to lighten uncomfortable situations. I had definitely never met anyone like him until I met his son, Joe, who's a Marx Brother in a little boy's body. Gotta love him!

I motioned for him to sit down, and I made him aware that his deceased mother had quite a lot to say.

"Rich, hurry up, your mom is talking to me. Come in so I can bring you up to speed."

Pad of paper in hand, I began scribbling vigorously (it's how I focus my energy), and a story started to unfold, telling me what kind of woman Rich's mom is. Let's just say, like mother, like son. And believe me, that's a huge compliment! His mom came through gushing about how proud she was of Rich, and how much she loves him and his family. She talked about liking Kristi, Rich's wife, very much, that she appreciated her sassy nature. His mom said she knew Rich would be a great dad one day, and she was right! There were a lot of messages given that day that meant a lot to Rich, and I was pleased to be able to do it. I was also glad to finally meet my friend's mom whom he loved so much and talked about with such affection.

Anyway, later that week I was on the air on KISS-FM to read call-in listeners (Johnjay and Rich are the morning show hosts on KISS-FM in Arizona). Only one day had passed since Rich's reading. Rich brought his reading up on the air to share with the listeners.

"Hey, Allison, remember in the reading you told me that my

mom wants my daughter Audrey to have her wedding ring?"

"Yeah, I remember."

"Well, when I left your house after the reading, I stopped by my mailbox to pick up the mail on my way home. In the mail was an envelope from my dad. I opened the envelope and my mom's wedding ring fell out of it!"

I mouthed "WOW!" I mean, what do you say to that?

I thought, "That's so great, the timing and all, and like I always say there are no coincidences."

Johnjay was totally stunned, which I find amusing. I never get tired of watching his jaw drop. He's always so surprised. He's like District Attorney Devalos on *Medium*; he never expects it, but it's kinda funny!

Rich was just floored, but really happy, too, and that's what mattered the most to me. Rich's mom did so well coming through. She had passed away when Rich was in his late teens. It had been a very long time, yet she managed to orchestrate things beautifully. I never question the Otherside about timing. There's always a reason why some things take longer than we'd like them to. Having faith will save your sanity; you don't waste so much time over-analyzing life.

Rich's Experience

It took me almost 20 years since the death of my mother, Audrey, to finally have the moment where we had a visit through Allison.

There are so many people who need closure, and so many aching to have that moment to finish relationships with those who have passed.

I had a rough ten years trying to forget about how bad it hurt to lose a parent, and needed another ten to get to a place where I could understand it.

I've known Al for such a long time, that I never thought to ask. And in typical "Allison fashion," she knew the right time to bring it up.

When I arrived at Allison's office, she ran to the door to greet me, and told me to come in. She already had pages and pages of notes, and wanted to get started.

I can tell you about all of the things she brought up in casual conversation that hit home, but that isn't what struck me.

The first thing I noticed when I walked into her office was that she seemed just like the people who used to hang around my mom.

It's hard to describe, but I felt like I was in a room where a little family reunion was taking place, and my mom was holding court.

My mom was a very peaceful and fun lady. There weren't many who escaped her quiet charm. Even as her kid, I noticed that people around her felt like they mattered, and they could really open up to her. I could see that Al had a good shot at connecting with my mom before I walked in.

What happened next was the closest thing to really getting to touch the Otherside that I've ever experienced.

This is the thing with Allison.

I have so many memories of my mom and our house that we grew up in. But this was different. Allison tapped into memories of this pastry my mom used to make that I totally forgot about.

She talked about a few moments after her death with my dad that not even he ever told me about.

I later got the nerve to grab my notes from the session and confirm with my dad the things Allison said were more than just a little accurate.

He had taken his time to get a headstone for my mother's grave, because he was in a lot of pain, and it seemed like too final of a burial to put in a headstone.

One of my aunts pulled him aside and helped him design one.

He spent a lot of time on making it look right, and made sure to put a rose in the corner. My mom was a devout Catholic, and her favorite saint was St. Theresa, who, if you prayed to for an answer, would show you a rose when your prayers had been heard by God.

That was my mom's favorite flower, and through Allison, she told me to say "Thank you" to my dad for the Rose. She said he would know what it meant.

He did.

I haven't heard my dad get choked up much, but he told me that was very real, and he told me that he now totally gets what Allison does.

She brought up relatives and moments and views that my mom has on my wife and children.

None of it gave me chills. It gave me warmth.

None of it was shocking. It was heartwarming.

It was like being at home around a fire at the holidays, having a nice conversation with the people you love the most. I could tell that my mom took a liking to Allison, and I could feel that it was sort of nice for Allison, too, as she dug deep and let herself go into my family. I know she deals with some very intense subject matter, and there is so much hurt out there.

Yes, I get sad sometimes that my mom isn't around to see my kids, or me following my dreams and sharing some success through a trip or a lunch at the beach, but I sort of always thought she was hanging around me and my kids. I always felt that now I had a pretty powerful angel leading me right just on the other side. Allison assured me that was the case.

I got confirmation on the fact that a body may give out, but your love for your family remains. Nothing as simple as a body dying can keep your soul away from the ones you love.

My Valentine

I was conducting a private reading for a woman named Judi whose husband, Mike, had passed away four years ago. He was the kind of guy that women pray to have in their life. Anyway, he came through so easily, and the reading was full of a lot of love and a trip down memory lane. Mike said to tell Judi that she would "always be his Valentine."

Judi then shared that her husband had died on Valentine's Day while having a heart transplant. I thought, "How terrible is that?"

Then Judi shared with me that she and her daughter had attended one of my events over a year ago, and I had read her daughter. "Oh really?" I thought, "That's good news!"

Allison, "You told my daughter that she was going to have a daughter, and she couldn't understand that because she had two boys. The doctor had told her that getting pregnant again could put her life in jeopardy, so her husband needed a vasectomy. After your event, her husband did just that, and soon after they found out that she was pregnant. Two days ago my daughter gave birth, to a baby girl, on Valentine's Day!"

The universe has a way of showing us that we're being taken care of, and when we physically lose someone who's a part of us, they have a way of sending us a new puzzle piece to add to our heart. That baby girl is a part of Mike, and no doubt she will bring much joy to their family.

Readings are mostly full of positive, uplifting tidbits of information that collectively makes up the story to someone's life, so try not to be afraid of the deceased or their messages. They're actually enjoyable moments that you are now familiar with since you've read this chapter.

Here's to wishing you a strong connection with those you love! Talk to them . . . they've been there all along.

Chapter 7

Children With The Gift

I'm often being asked about children with the gift, even though some people don't see it as a gift, and some children might agree with those people. I'd like to beg to differ, and explain how the gift is very much influenced by our personality and environment.

Joe and I have three daughters who have been brought up in an open household, understanding of individuality and beauty being in the eye of the beholder. As I know everybody has a unique take on how they see one another, and as long as we respect our differences and agree to disagree, everything can be quite harmonious. I was a child who talked to the souls who remained after physical death. I liked them. They made me feel protected. And believe me, I was very protected.

It was the 1970's and 80's when I was a pint-size medium. Things were different then; people didn't embrace children who talked to spirits. I was no exception. I now have three daughters with the ability to do the same, but they were brought up in a teaching environment with me as their teacher. I saw their raw abilities from the age of two on, and as they grew I began to help them strengthen and hone their skills. I tried to make it fun for them, like a game. They're very competitive, and they were incredibly good in the "classroom."

As the girls get older, their vocabulary expands and their life experiences increase, and this gives the deceased a greater chance to communicate through them, because they have more overlapping life experiences to draw from. In other words, if a child can't spell "Canada," they'd have a hard time conveying the country most important to the deceased, because they don't have the reference to recognize "Canada" when the word pops into their head. Just like a small child could get "red car" but not "red Corvette," because they have no reference for Corvette. So, as the gifted age, they get stronger because they're more relatable to a wider age range of deceased, as a result of their increasing life experiences.

For the first time, my girls will share with you in their own words their advice for young people who have the special ability to hold hands with those who have passed. I feel like since I give those I read a chance to share their stories with those who can relate, that maybe my girls also need to share their advice with those who need someone to relate to. In my book, *Don't Kiss Them Good-bye*, I share some of my own childhood experiences. Now you will hear from the next generation in their own words . . . my three girls.

Our oldest daughter, Aurora, is a cheerleader, and she does the entertainment news for her high school's TV news station. She's an over-achiever, and we're very proud of her. We're just getting used to her driving, and she goes to college next year, so we're trying to enjoy our time with her while she's home. Aurora's super intelligent, like Joe. She's stunning and sarcastic. I don't know where she got the sarcasm from; Joe and I fight over taking credit for that quality!

Aurora's Advice (16-years-old)

"Practicing with my friend Amanda Campbell helps me to strengthen and improve my abilities, because if you don't practice, your intuition gets dull. You don't need a Ouija Board to connect with the Otherside—just a pad of paper and a pencil to write down the messages coming through. Sometimes it feels like you're guessing, because it is occasionally too easy, or at least it seems so."

Our daughter, Fallon, is in junior high, and she has a gorgeous voice. For her birthday, she wants an electric guitar to pair with her voice. She loves to bake, just like my grandma Jenee, and she's a talented baker at that! Fallon is an electronics guru and digs movies and TV. Fallon's the kind of girl who doesn't like pink, and she can hang with boys just as easy as other girls. She's a lot of fun to be around, and she's a hugger. She's a very loving kid.

Fallon's advice (13-years-old)

"Make sure you're in a quiet place, and writing down the name of the person who died helps me to connect. When a name, picture or song pops in your head, write it down so you don't forget what came through in the reading. That way you have time to make sense of your information.

When I feel overwhelmed at night, if there's activity around me, I like to roll myself up in a comfy blanket. It soothes me.

I remember being in art class, and we were supposed to make an animal out of paper. I couldn't think of anything, and then a "beaver" popped into my head. Christmas rolled around and I gave it to my mom's friend, Laurie Campbell. She started crying and said that when her dad was dying he was hallucinating, and he kept talking about seeing a beaver sitting by a pond, and it calmed him. She said my gift made her really happy, like it was her dad saying he was okay. I was drawn to give it to Laurie, and now I know it's because her dad was telling me, too. Cool!"

Sophia is our youngest daughter. She's "the baby," and she owns that title. She's very active. She's a competitive cheerleader and all-around jock. She loves flag football, basketball—you name it! She was born on the Fourth of July, and is an all-American girl. Sophia's a little comedian. She's very sensitive, and fiercely loyal. People just love her.

Sophia's Advice (11-years-old)

"When bringing through family members (spirits), I'm not scared because they're related to me, so maybe only stick to the people closest to you and your parents to bring through. Only share your information with family, not with classmates, because they don't always understand and it can make it kind of weird to be around them later. If your parents don't understand either, then write what information you hear and see down in your diary. It helps you to release the energy."

Joe and I also have "family game night' with the girls, and we saw it as a valuable tool to teach them how to trust their first instinct. In this case, we played "Loaded Questions" (a card game sold in toy stores). The point of the game is to know by how the players answered a question, who it was that contributed each answer to your question. We were able to show the girls that whenever they second-guessed themselves, they lost points. When they trusted their gut-instinct, they gained points. So we practiced until they became comfortable trusting their first instinct. If you think about it, we have to be programmed to trust and rely on ourselves. You'd think that would come naturally, but we've become comfortable relying on another person's opinion or insight, rather than our own. I guess it's sort of the "grass is always greener on the other side of the fence" scenario.

Trusting your first instinct does actually have to be self-taught, because unfortunately, as we get older, our head gets filled with alternate opinions, and critical thinking becomes our new method. Over-analysis seems to be second nature to all of us Type "A" personalities, as well as those who doubt themselves.

It was nice sitting down and asking my girls what advice they would give to other kids who were dealing with having the gift in childhood. Our daughters are in a unique position, having Joe and me as parents, as well as having a voice to help others like them.

Lilydale

Lilydale is a town in New York that is constructed of mediums. Yes, you have to be a medium to live there, and every summer they open their doors to the public. In the summer of 2008, I agreed to give a children's seminar there to help the very young mediums out there to hone their skills. Joe and I decided to bring our girls so they could really soak in the experience and play with kids "like them."

We arrived in Lilydale on a Tuesday morning, and it was pouring rain, I mean POURING. We pulled up in front of the Lyceum Hall where my event was being held. Joe and I were promptly met at our car by a sweet man who introduced himself as "Teddy." He ushered us through the rain with a wonderful smile on his face, as if the day was sunny and bright. I entered the Lyceum and cast my gaze upon 52 shining young faces whose eyes struck me as nervous. Me, make people nervous? Never! (I'm kidding; I seem to have that effect on people.) I capped the attendance at 50, so that I could have personal time with the kids, where they each got my full attention.

I immediately broke the kids into five groups of ten kids, and arranged them in circles. The kids ranged in age from 5 to 18, both boys and girls. I stood before the kids and I began to speak to them about my own experiences in childhood. I talked about naming my stuffed animals after the deceased friends and family members who lingered in my room. It's important that kids with abilities have the security of feeling like they have a physical object filling the area that is inhabited. If they don't have to worry about turning around and being caught off-guard by an entity, then their nerves fare better.

As I recounted my childhood to these kids, I realized that I grew up to be a teacher. Huh! That surprised me and thrilled me all at the same time. I went on to describe getting bored in church when I was small, like most kids do. When a psychic gets bored sometimes, our minds wander and start "pulling impressions" off of those sitting near us. This story received chuckles from the kids as they looked at me with crooked smiles and eyes of mischief. I loved it!

Many of the kids spoke of "shadowy figures" that frighten them. I thought I should touch on this in my book, since it seems so common. When you see a shadowy figure up close or out of the corner of your eye, don't assume it's negative. Many shadowy figures appear as such, because they don't want to frighten their living loved ones. In other words, if they were to speak to you or appear as an apparition, they fear scaring us. They stay in the shadows trying to stay around us, without interfering with our lives. So please, if you see a shadowy figure, consider it might be someone who loves you, or a person in your family who didn't know you in life, but chooses to protect you in death.

So the class continued as I answered their questions and empathized with their confusion. I described to them what "cancer" feels like to me when I encounter a spirit who had it, or a living person who presently does. I described what a heart attack feels like to a medium, so they could recognize it, too. I explained that if a name comes through in their mind, a first name will "feel" BOLD, and a middle name feels somewhat REMOVED, less powerful, and that's how they can determine the difference between a middle name and a first one.

After I was done answering questions, I had my assistant, Andrea, hand out notepads and pens to the kids, and I told them they were going to "READ" each other. Their little mouths formed perfect "O's," and they seemed hesitant. I told them not to be afraid to be wrong.

I said, "The world is our classroom, we don't have the luxury of years of formal schooling to be mediums."

It's thrust upon us, and that's okay. But to "misread" a sign or communication from the Otherside is human error, and with practice accuracy increases. When you become a full-fledged medium, with practice and trial and error, you become very certain that what you're receiving is factual, even if the client says no. You learn to hold onto the Otherside and stick with your information, and after a couple of minutes the client realizes you're right. Sometimes readings can be overwhelming, and the client isn't connecting the dots in their head. A medium's information needs to settle in, and the light bulb then seems to go on in the client's head. This moment is what I refer to as "a meeting of the mind and soul."

Here's an example from one of my events, so that you have a specific account of what I mean when I say a "meeting of the mind and soul":

I did a reading at one of my events that I thought would be an encouraging learning experience for people with abilities. I brought a man up on stage with me who was clearly missing his partner who had passed 19 years prior, but the pain was very much still part of his fabric. During the reading, I delivered messages and gave him the information that I "saw" connected to his partner. There were a couple of details that didn't resonate with him, but I told him to just "bank it" and think about it later. One of the details that I kept getting was the name "Carlos," connected to the deceased, and "Mexico." He really wasn't sure what it meant. Two days later at another event, a woman who had attended the event said, "After the readings ended, I was talking to the gentleman that you read, and he told me that he had forgotten that his partner's middle name was "Carlos," and his partner was born in Mexico.

This is common. It happens all the time, really, because when people are being read, it can be overwhelming, and they have trouble connecting the dots. I shared this reading snippet for those of you who have abilities, so that you remember to stand by your information received in a reading. "Sitters" need time to process the information, so don't take it personally if they can't confirm your information on the spot. Just move on and keep moving forward with the reading.

Another common occurrence in a room full of people is having a reading "hijacked." During one event, a woman wanted to hear from her mom, and the woman sitting next to her had also lost her mom, and she ended up hijacking the reading. The mother energy kept showing me what looked like a soda fountain with a long counter and young people sitting on stools. She then said, "She loved birds," that they were symbolic of her and would visit her daughters often. This meant nothing to the original sitter. The woman sitting next to her began to sob, so I asked if she was okay. She said she was, and that she had a picture of her mom sitting at a long counter in what looks like a soda fountain back in the day, and it was prominently displayed in her house. Also, her mom loved birds and she "knew" they were sent by her mom, so she knew she was still there. I brought through her dad, as well. He was a hoot. Needless to say, she and her sister loved the reading, and they were very happy.

For those who practice in groups, be careful, because it's

the "strongest" energy that will come through and be heard, so make sure to explain this to your group before you start. And remember to not be stubborn, but if in your gut you know your information is true and correct, stand by it with respect for your sitter, and move on to the next part of the reading.

Life Experience

It's important for gifted kids to know that the more life experience you have, the bigger the pool of reference you have to work with in readings. For instance, my friend, Laurie Campbell, who's a phenomenal medium, grew up in a family-owned hair salon, so when she does readings, she can get whether or not the deceased had permed hair, dyed hair, what the texture was, etc. I grew up in a family where food was very important to show affection, and the time was invested in making unforgettable meals. When I do a reading, I have a knack at describing the food the deceased cooked or the food they enjoyed eating. We know that often the living "love" through food (some of us are called "feeders" or "foodies"), and our kids/grandkids feel special when we make them a favorite treat. So you can understand why, in a reading, family dishes are often acknowledged. The kids seemed to understand this. I told them to see the world and read a lot, and that'll give them a great database for the deceased to access.

As the kids raised their pens to do as I instructed them to (which was "write the impressions that you pull off of someone in your group"), I felt a sense of pride. I was proud of them, and I felt like any mother hearing her child say their first word. As I moved from group to group, I saw most children thrive, and a few retreat. Some of the kids received verified names connected to their peers, and some decided to retreat into a world that would remain most likely unknown to them. I saw this as no different from grown mediums that I've encountered in my life. (I mean no disrespect by that observation.)

Some personalities are fighters, and they approach challenges with competitive spirit and open minds. Other personalities are "meek" energy that shy away from conflict and challenges, because it's not in their energy to take a chance and possibly fail. That's okay, because sometimes time has a way of toughening us up so we can rise to the occasion when it's our calling. And sometimes energy is soft, and not meant for challenges. All energies have some purpose.

It was dazzling seeing the kids who had strong abilities rise to the occasion, and you could see it click in their head when they were told they were right about the information they delivered in their reading. That was followed by a big grin and an occasional high-five. My family really enjoyed our time with all of the children. They were special sparks of light. I hope the tools that I gave them will help them to strengthen their instincts and connect with the Otherside.

Life is about timing, courage, and heart that will elevate your soul to understand exactly what your calling might be. Recognizing a calling is something that many never figure out, because they look too hard. A person might own a bakery for 40 years and feel that they made no difference in the world, but if they pull back and take a broader look, they will see their life for what it really was. They had a store that children rushed to after school for a cookie, and it raised their spirits. It gave them something to look forward to, and years later to tell their own children about.

The baker made wedding cakes and 50th anniversary cakes that celebrated the wonder of life we all know as love. When somebody died, a mourner would pass the store and pick up a peach pie for the wake that reminded the widow of how much her husband loved her pies, and it made her smile. The baker was a constant reminder of life needing to be celebrated, and he was indeed adored by many people. If he's a wise man he will recognize this, and if he looked too closely and didn't realize it in life, then he learned it after his passing. Either way, he touched those drawn to him and his family. Look at your life, take a step back and see what a miracle you can be to others. It's never too late to be someone's miracle.

So don't give up. You have to strive for excellence in whatever you do in life, otherwise you settle for mediocrity. Some people say, "I flip burgers. Why should I work to be excellent at that?" Well, because it won't take long for you to be elevated to something better, because a positive attitude is unfortunately more rare. I know people who worked at theme parks and were singled out to be personal assistants, and then elevated to be producers in television. So never question that people are watching you; often they're the people whom you want to attract. A sense of humor, a great attitude, and not being a complainer will get you far. Oh yeah, and don't forget FAITH in yourself.

TV Kids

I was asked to be on a talk show to act as an expert on children with abilities. I guess I qualify: I have three little girls with gifts, and I was a little girl at one time eons ago.

The pulse of New York City is exhilarating and the dreamers come in steady streams every day. The possibilities in that wondrous city are endless, and the food . . . well, don't get me started—ridiculously good.

I was a little nervous, since I had never been on a show sharing the stage with kids before, and I wasn't sure of what to expect. The show was high energy, and that included the dance music during commercial breaks that had a bass that practically bounced me out of my chair. The kids on the show loved it though, and they were out of their chairs dancing and singing, really soaking in the moment.

I observed the girls, and listened to their stories about seeing how other kids' cruelty had left an impression on them that they'd carry for life. I told them the next time someone accused them of being "the devil," tell them if they really believed you were the devil, they wouldn't dare say so, because you could pop their head in half. We all snickered knowing how absurd a statement it is to think we are somehow the Anti-Christ. We spend our lives helping people, nothing a bad person would do with their abilities.

Anyway, the kids seemed relieved and refreshed to be standing with an older version of themselves. I noted how lucky they are to have each other to turn to, since I had a different generation to quarrel with. I was ecstatic to be present in a time where spirituality had become so universal and commonplace.

There were several girls present with various abilities. I gave them each a pad of paper and a pencil. I selected a few people out of the audience for them to attempt to write the impressions they got connected to, whomever they felt drawn to. Most of the girls were too distracted to write, or just were drawing a blank.

There were a few girls, however, who were very able to "automatic write" like I do. It's not for everybody, and it doesn't mean you have no abilities if you can't do it. It helps me in sorting and holding onto the impressions that come through to me. One of the little girl's "Ahli's" letters and numbers were just like the ones I write (meaning tracing each letter 25 times or so, making it large and profound-looking). She had written "mom" and "3," so I told her there were a couple of ways to interpret the information.

I said, "Ask the lady if she's the mom of three kids."

When we asked the woman if she was a mom of three, she said, "Yes." I high-fived the little girl, and told her she should be very proud of herself. She looked surprised at her talent, and I was just so tickled inside to have been able to help her find another tool to sharpen her skills.

All of the little girls were very special and individual, and I enjoyed meeting them very much. When we were done, I allowed each volunteer to ask me a question, since they were so generous to allow the kids to practice on them. I went down the line (there were about 8 people) and I read them all (letting them each ask one question that's important to them) within 10 minutes, wished them well, and exited. I had told the girls that if they kept practicing, they too, would be able to systematically read many people one after the other, disconnecting quickly, and that would help them if they ever do radio readings or group readings in the future. They seemed pretty happy to hear that.

I went back to my green room and one-by-one the girls came back to talk to me for a moment and receive a signed copy of my book, *Secrets of the Monarch*. I have a lot of love for those little girls who choose to lay it on the line in front of a television camera every week on their show. However, I'm not sure it's good for them at such a young age. I'm a "Momma Bear," and I like to protect my kids, all kids from growing up too fast. I'm grown and I know the pressures tied to filming our abilities. Even when you do mind-blowing readings, you still deal with the warped individuals who are full of angst and hate and feel self-entitled to dictate an arena they know nothing about. I constantly remind myself that those people "don't get" spirituality right now, but they still have room to grow through their own life experiences. Those who continue to evolve spiritually in this lifetime will reap the benefits in the Afterlife.

I realize that it's the children who are most vital to nurture. They are our future, they usher in heightened awareness. So, I occasionally do children's workshops to help them fast-forward their abilities. We live in a society where everyone wants to be right, and that's more important than learning to some. We need to fix that. We all need to live our truth and not condemn others for doing the same, as long as they respect our boundaries.

It's easy to pontificate to others about what's right and wrong. It's much harder to open yourself up to listening and taking in what people are trying to share with you. We should all learn from one another. Balance is the key in life. Find your balance, where what you do for others unselfishly should at least equal what gifts we gratefully receive from the Universe . . . and we receive plenty.

My Children

I think we should all learn something from both the parents and children in these powerful stories of love and connection. Just because someone doesn't live a long life, doesn't render them any less powerful. Their souls are constructed of great emotion, and they crave to remain present in their family picture.

Children are so strong both in life and the Afterlife because they aren't jaded, and they don't over-intellectualize like we adults often do, and then we miss the point.

Earlier in the book I shared some powerful and touching stories of children coming through from the Afterlife. Now I want to share my experience as a mother of three gifted daughters bringing through their own family members. From time to time I teach my girls my methods in readings, and I look at their individual personalities, and how that coincides with their abilities.

One of my girlfriends was in town, and her father had recently passed away. I sat my girls down at the patio table on our back porch. I placed a blank piece of paper in front of each of the three girls. I told them the first name of the man who had passed and nothing more, and had them write his name at the top of their paper. I let them know that it doesn't matter if they get it wrong, because it's all part of learning how to trust your instincts. Some information can be hard to put into words, and it takes practice. Some information is highly unusual, and you have to "stick to your guns," and not override your inner voice with your mind, just because it's unfamiliar information. Often it's the obscure information that means the most.

My daughters told me they were nervous because they didn't want to disappoint me if they weren't good at it. I assured them that I love them, and their ability level would never impact my love for them, and to just give it a try.

I have to tell you that I went into this experience expecting just about anything from them, ranging from not being good at automatic writing to being great, but not interested.

I sat back with my friend and watched my girls begin writing down their impressions connected to the deceased as they drew them in. After a few minutes, I asked them to share some of what they wrote down with me. Our oldest, Aurora, surprised herself with the accuracy of her information, and blew my friend away. Fallon kept naming songs connected to the deceased. (This is what I mentioned earlier in how our personality shapes our style of reading.) She listens to music all the time, so she's particularly good at playing "Name that Tune" with the Afterlife.

Sophia, our youngest said, "He says he's connected to Canada and New York. They're important to him." She sounded like me when I read—I was so proud! My friend confirmed that her dad went to college in Canada, and they took a very mean-ingful trip there together. My friend smiled at Sophia and told her how significant her information was. Sophia was beaming!

Then she told my daughter that her dad had been born in New York, and that her reading made a lot of sense. My girl gets locations, yes! Not bad for an eleven-year-old girl. Some medi-ums are average or not so good at locations, so this was cool to me, since it's one of my own strong points, as well. They were the only locations she named, and both were pivotal in the qual-ity of the reading.

Later, the girls brought through Joe's dad whom unfortu-nately they had not met, since he passed away before they were born. Joe was a good lesson for them. I know he won't take offense by this, but he was not a very good "sitter." He'll get more aware with practice and greatly improve.

I stepped in and bridged the gap between the girls and Joe during the reading. Aurora kept hearing her granddad talk about the "red T-shirt." Joe was like, "No, that doesn't ring a bell with me."

I turned to him and said, "Joe, don't you have your dad's red T-shirt balled-up at the top of our closet? I remember seeing it years ago."

Joe looked at me, and it was like a light bulb went on in his head. "Oh yeah, the one that says, "I Pay The Bills" in white lettering."

This is a great example of how when another family member is present, it can be helpful, because they're not as invested in the reading as the person being read, and usually are better with recall. The girls all gave great details connected to Joe's dad, and we were both impressed and so very proud of them.

They pushed their papers toward me, and I found it extraordinary that when I lined their papers up side-by-side, their information was in triplicate. Joe and I had sat right across from them at the table. There was no peeking at their sister's paper going on; they just all "received" overlapping information. Out of approximately 25 pieces of information, 20 parts of each of our three girls' readings were identical, when we compared all three of their papers. Pretty cool! It demonstrates that Joe's dad had specific things he needed heard by Joe, and all three granddaughters were simply listening to their granddad and "taking notes."

Tips for Parents

Some of my best tips for parents with gifted children are quite simple. Letting your child know that they can tell you ANYTHING is key. Remember, kids can feel it if you don't believe them, so being sincerely supportive is necessary. For parents without abilities, be prepared to hear things that may seem "out there" to you. Your child might see angels that they will describe as tall and somber-looking. Angels have very positive energy, but they're also warriors, so they can appear to be intimidating in size and demeanor. They act as protection, especially to children.

Another strange sighting can be what I call "mischievous" energy, and as far as I can tell, they were living pranksters that still like stirring up trouble. I saw one of these once. It was a cloudy white color and would wrap its head around the corner and peek at me, and then faster than humanly possible pull its head back, so I couldn't see it anymore. It just kept repeating this over and over. My mantra to block these entities involves asking the Otherside to "block any negative or mischievous entities from me and my family, not allowing them to be around us or come in contact with us." This has always worked for me, and I highly recommend it.

A child is never too young to see something supernatural. My kids were two or three-years-old when they started communicating to Joe and me that they were seeing spirits. So, if you have a really young child telling you that they see a person in their room, believe them.

Kids at that age are already hesitant to tell people what they observed, because they're not really sure what they're seeing, so it's hard for them to articulate what they saw.

Children are a big draw for spirits, because they are the brightest of energies, and the deceased love to be around them. Especially infants, they like to make funny faces at them and make them laugh. I think babies are the closest in energy to spirits because they have no chip on their shoulder or issues. Once a child is old enough to draw, you can ask them to draw a picture of the person they see, and the images that the spirit shows your child. It's like Kindergarten automatic writing with crayons—I love it!

As gifted children get older, let them practice on you, pull impressions off of you. This is okay as long as it's open to family or friends. I tell our kids not to talk about what we do at school because not everybody can see what we see. For little kids, just tell them they have "special eyes" that see what some people can't. Most importantly, let them know that what they can do is a good thing; it's not bad or strange, but very normal amongst feeling beings. Animals can sense the Otherside because they use their instincts all the time, so sensing spirits is second nature to them. Kids also have heightened energy because they are emotionally based, like spirits. As they get older, it's important to make sure they continue to trust their instincts. One day it may save their life.

An exercise that I do with our kids is I throw out the name of a relative who died long ago, and I have them write it at the top of their pad of paper. I let them practice pulling impressions off of the name, and let them know how proud I am of them. Sometimes you have to fact-check their information with an older generation, and sometimes you won't be able to verify what they got, but that doesn't mean they're wrong, either. Sometimes the details will seem obscure, but often those are the most special pieces to the puzzle. When treated as a game, it's actually fun to do. Our kids are always amazed at how accurate and straightforward their information is. So am I, and a proud Mama Bear.

The information they get should be mostly positive, and if their information is mostly dark and negative, then you have to look at other possibilities rather than psychic/mediumship tendencies. A child's personality is going to factor into how they process the information they receive, as well as how they interact with spirits. This is the same for grown mediums, too. If you have a funny, light-hearted child, they will pull positive, fun family members from the Otherside. Even the deceased who were grumpy in life are able to share their lighter energy with an upbeat kid.

A child who has temper issues or acts out negatively regularly will draw dark energy to them, because like attracts like. In essence, they speak the same language. So, kids who talk about mostly the dark stuff may have some underlying personal problems that are going to be made worse by their gift acting as a portal to negative entities. Addressing behavioral problems or depression in a child will help them to hopefully heal and shift their energy, which will give them focus, allowing their abilities to act as a gift—not a curse. The healthier and happier the child, the greater their potential will be to become a phenomenal psychic/medium in adulthood.

Parents, when you're working with your kids, keep in mind that by you being open to their abilities, you will begin to see more of your own. So play the games with them, and work on not dismissing it when you're right about one of the cards or an impression, or more likely that you'll "get" the same impression as your child at exactly the same time.

With little girls or little boys, you can use something as simple as a Barbie to teach them. Tell your child to close their eyes. Then pick an outfit for the doll and hide it behind your back. Tell them to visualize what color outfit you chose. If it's too hard for them, just have them tell you if the color feels warm or cold. This can help them learn red (warm) or blue (cold). It really does help them determine colors, and that is very important in readings. It's how we know the color of the deceased's clothing, their hair color, etc. They don't always show us their image; sometimes they have to convey color through feeling. For me, black comes through as a "hard" feeling, like a blacktop; white comes through as a "soft" feeling, like a cloud.

Keep in mind that everyone has their own style, but that's how it works for me. It's also fun to play the game with food. If they can tell you the color of the treat that's covered in the bowl, they can have it. Use several treats, because we don't want any children starving. It can be as simple as a grape or strawberry for this game.

Helping your kids to realize their talents is one of the most loving gestures that you can make as a parent. Love your children unconditionally, and tell them often that they are special, and you're so glad that they are yours.

Chapter 8

Walking Through Time

Tombstone

As the fingers of the past strummed the strings of my life, I realized Tombstone had to be hit head on. Not for ratings or another's gratification, but for me, because Tombstone is where I believe I may have been before. I've always felt connected to Tombstone. It's always felt familiar to me and I've always felt living energy around me while in that town. I felt like there was dust on my feet, guilt on my mind, and unfinished business in my heart. So I figured, why not? Why not go there and see what happens, and what I feel?

So, me, a medium in Tombstone . . . what would it bring? An Answer? A conflict? Would I be personally disappointed? There was only one way for me to find out exactly why I felt pulled there. So it was settled, a Tombstone adventure was on the horizon. None of us know for sure why we relate to another time and place, but don't we owe it to ourselves to find out?

August 25, 2008

I have been asked by many ghost-hunting teams to accompany them to haunted locations before, and I had always respectfully declined. The reason is that I don't want cameras stuck in my face distracting me from the personal experience that I so crave in historical places. If I'm going out to communicate with historical ghosts, I'm doing it on my terms, nobody else's.

In 2005, I heard from a ghost-hunter named Terry Fisk, and his partner Chad Lewis, who are paranormal investigators for Unexplained Research LLC. They were both nice guys trying to understand the paranormal without a political agenda, or a need to "cash in" like scientists from my past experiences (who must really love me because they're still obsessing over me). God bless! No, Terry and Chad simply wanted me to look at their book on haunted locations and see what I thought. I was happy to do so, and it was a wonderful guide to haunted locations, by the way. For all those amateur ghost-hunters out there, the book includes some very "active" destinations.

In 2008, I decided to call them and invite them to meet me in Tombstone, Arizona, where Doc Holiday and Wyatt Earp became famous for trying to establish law, and where the infamous fight at the O.K. Corral took place. Terry Fisk was committed to being there, and brought his dad, Larry, for a haunted vacation. I brought my good friend, Jaena Moynihan, who's also a medium. We were psyched about taking a girl's road trip, so I packed my Willie Nelson, Kenny Rogers and Bob Seger CD's and we hit the road ready for whomever and whatever awaited us—living or otherwise.

I booked the "Rose Room" at the Silver Nugget Hotel that faces the famous Bird Cage Saloon. It's the only room I'll stay in when I'm in town. It just "feels" inhabited in a very cool way. It's not fancy, but it's real and a sort of "time machine" during your stay.

The room also has a deck overlooking the Birdcage, and you can sit and play poker out there while tourists hustle back and forth in the street down below.

The first time I saw Terry Fisk was from the back walking down the dusty road that ran down the center of town. He was walking with his delightful dad, Larry, and two members of his team, Dawnette and Tammy. I called to him, "Hey, Terry, Allison DuBois. How are you doing?"

Terry was quirky. He reminded me of Dan Akroyd in the movie Ghostbusters. He was really knowledgeable and had a real passion for his work. He also had an inner light that was ob-vious, and he was approachable as well as friendly. His dad was excited and happy to be in Tombstone. I think the town brings out the inner bad child in people. Dawnette was a little brunette who was a girl-next-door sort with a fantastic laugh. Tammy had the energy of a twenty-year-old, and that was apparent when I'd crack a joke and she'd laugh lightening hearts all around her. She had light blonde hair that looked like summer. All four were easy to like and be around.

After brief introductions, they asked where I'd like to start. I was immediately drawn to the courthouse, maybe because I've always felt a kinship with the law . . . maybe because it was the strongest concentration of spirit activity in Tombstone. The courthouse was the heart of the town where people lived and died by the law. So we started there. The courthouse was closed, so we gave Terry the impressions we received from the outside of the building, figuring we'd fact-check them the following day.

We decided to walk to the courthouse in the early morning when apparently there's quite a lot of spirit activity, according to paranormal investigators. Walking through Tombstone early in the morning felt as though we'd been transported back to 1885. I felt very anxious as well as very excited. There was a distinct feeling of fear, as well, which I'm not used to feeling from spirits. I could, however, be picking up on impressions left behind from gunfights that occurred long ago. When we approached the courthouse I looked up and saw a judge in a particular upstairs window with a black derby, a beard, and round wire glasses.

The following day, we all went up to that window, the one in the courtroom. Next to it was a picture of the judge whom I had described, round glasses and all. I also saw little boys trying to look around the corner to watch prisoners being lead to the noose. I could see a man of the cloth there for prayer for the condemned man's soul. Between Jaena and I, we painted the picture of an execution day through our information that the Otherside was facilitating for us. We were having an amazing time sampling the past. Again, I went there to enjoy myself, and I was enjoying it all!

Earlier, we had gone to the Birdcage Saloon at midnight, and had some interesting interactions with those who choose to remain there, tapping into the impressions left behind in the building from past occurrences. It was a little disheartening, because in the rooms where the prostitutes "did their business" I could hear them screaming from certain "surgical" procedures. I could see a cowboy sitting at the poker table that was roped off, and he kept waving me over to his table to sit with him; he must have thought I was there to "work." It's a different time now, and I'm not that kind of girl. It was still amusing to me, though. I couldn't help but to chuckle knowing that this "cowboy" wanted my company.

For us, being there at midnight was like a "Haunted Disney-land" for a medium. What a one-of-a-kind experience. Our host warned us to watch out for the whiptail scorpions. That statement had me jumping around to make sure I had a clear view of the floor! Scary! I don't care for scorpions, and I like to keep my distance whenever possible. I enjoyed seeing all of Terry's tools and gizmos for measuring energy and spirits. It was definitely a memorable experience that I hope to repeat someday.

Terry Fisks account of Tombstone

When I talk about my experience with Allison DuBois in Tombstone at my speaking engagements and conferences, it brings me back to a most interesting interlude with a town with a lot of history, and the first time I met Allison.

I make sure to explain to people that the courthouse is now a museum, but when we first arrived there it had already closed for the day. So, we walked about the outside of the courthouse museum, and Allison gave me some of her impressions connected to the property. She pointed to a window on the first floor and said, "Inside that room I sense the handling of money."

At the time, this didn't seem to make much sense to me, as this used to be a courthouse, not a bank.

We walked to the opposite side of the building where there was a huge brick wall with a locked gate. The wall was too high to see what was on the other side, but she said she sensed gallows and hangings that took place there in the 1800's. Since I couldn't see what was on the other side of the wall, I didn't know if this was accurate or not. Then Allison pointed to a window on the second floor and she said she could see a judge looking out the window. Allison said he was wearing a black derby and wire-framed glasses, he had a white beard, and sported a little black bow tie. I looked up at the window, but I didn't see anybody.

Being skeptical, the next day I returned to the museum after the doors had opened. I went to the room where she sensed the handling of money and noticed a sign that indicated it used to be the county treasurer's office. I went inside the room and found a huge walk-in vault that wasn't visible from outside the window. Her psychic impression seemed to be right on the money (no pun intended).

After that, I walked to the back of the courthouse and out the back door to see what was behind the brick wall. Lo and behold, I discovered a gallows with a historic marker that detailed the hangings that took place on that very spot in the 1800's.

I went back into the courthouse, up to the second floor, and to the window where she saw a judge looking out. I didn't see anybody standing there, but I did notice some historic photos on the wall. One of these photos was of Judge James F. Duncan. Judge Duncan was a county judge in Tombstone for 36 years. He had served longer than any other Cochise County judge had ever served. I would assume that the courthouse had become quite the home for the judge, after all he spent quite a lot of time there. Then I took a closer look at the picture of Judge Duncan and noticed he had a black derby, wire-frame glasses, a white beard, and a little black bow tie—just like the ghost she saw looking out of the window!

Final Thought

I'd like to thank Terry Fisk and his dad, Larry Fisk, for being such good sports and tackling Tombstone with me. I know I can be a handful sometimes. I truly loved the experience, and one day I will do it again!

Interpreter

I am often asked, "Are there language barriers for mediums if the deceased speaks a different language?"

Here is my answer to that very solid question.

I took my family with me to Tokyo for a *Medium* TV Series/book tour. I hadn't anticipated the events that would follow my arrival. Joe had asked me where I had wanted to go while in Tokyo. Please don't think me too morbid, but I felt drawn to the cemetery where the 47 Ronin Warriors were buried. The story of the Samurai who had avenged the death of their lord fascinated me, and I wanted to walk their sacred grounds. Also, I wanted to take our girls to a Japanese Tea Ceremony, so that my girls could learn of Japanese traditions and their respect for one another.

When our plane landed early in the morning in Tokyo my jet-lagged family of five was promptly greeted at the airport by an effervescent young man named Fumi. He was our interpreter.

Fumi was an energy ball of a young man who also happened to moonlight as a saxophone player. From the get-go, it was clear that Fumi was going to be an outrageously interesting guide to have on our first trip to this beautiful country. Fumi was excited to be our host/interpreter for the trip, and our girls would end up growing very attached to him by the conclusion of our tour. Fumi had lived in Boston for a few years chasing his dream of playing his saxophone for large audiences in a jazz band. Since he had lived in America for quite some time, his English was good, and he was eager to absorb some of our American slang terms. Our daughter, Aurora, fed him a large helping of slang. His favorites were "Copy that" and "Right on!"

Anyway, I had a busy schedule with media, but was given a day and a half to acclimate to the sixteen-hour time difference, and that was a good thing. My first day was packed with interviews, and I was introduced to my interpreter who would assist me with translating my English into Japanese for the press. She was strangely familiar to me, as if we'd met before. Her name was Mari. She was tall and slender making her appear very feminine, yet with a commanding presence. Mari had a smile that was reassuring, and ever-present to lift the spirit of any stranger. She had delicate features, but in her eyes you could see that she also had an iron inner-strength that grew from being worldly, as well as clearing many obstacles in her life with precision. She was a world-class interpreter who was used to interpreting for stars such as Bruce Willis when the entertainment world came knocking. I never had to repeat myself once to Mari, she had it down; she was my "one-take wonder."

There was a buzz in the air in the press room, and I would

do well over twenty interviews in a day. These were long days, and I did this for several days. Although it was a lot of work, and I might still be a little scarred (just kidding), what made it really great was the people and how engaging they were. They had a natural curiosity in learning about the Otherside, as well as learning about my family.

When I sat down with Mari and one of the many reporters, I could feel her mother and grandmother's presence. So to acknowledge them, I mentioned them hypothetically when speaking to Mari. When I had an opportunity to use them in an example, I did so as I spoke to Mari and the reporter. The description of my examples of interaction with the Otherside were specific to what Mari's mother and grandmother were showing me. Joe knows that in an abstract sort of way, I frequently will use the information coming through to me as an example directed at the person whom it is intended for. I do this to not overstep my bounds, but still give the essence of the message to the living, leaving them thinking of their loved one and opening them up to the possibility that the message was connected to them.

Mari looked surprised when she heard my example, but continued in a professional manner, occasionally glancing over at me with question marks in her eyes. At the end of the interview we cleared the air, and I explained to her why I had mentioned her mom and grandma. She acknowledged them as being the two closest people to her whom she had lost. She was very happy to hear that they had such a strong presence in her life, and that they were with her daily. So the bond between Mari and I had begun. It was the beginning of a chain of events that would leave us both speechless.

Joe received my itinerary and informed me that the following Sunday I was set to visit the Ronin Cemetery on my first day off following the press tour. I apologized to Joe that it fell on Father's Day. He assured me that the history lesson would surely be fascinating, no matter what day it fell on.

Mari and I would eventually do somewhere around thirty interviews together. It was a lot, but would no doubt be well worth it launching *Medium* in Japan.

During one of the interviews, I was given another opportunity to pass information to Mari from her mother in the form of an example for the press. Mari's mom kept talking about her pearl ring that Mari had, and I relayed the object to Mari. She smiled at me and I could see that she was moved. After the interview was over, Mari shared with me that she was going to wear her mom's pearl ring to the interviews that day, but then opted not to. I told Mari that her mom was letting her know that even without the ring on her hand, her mom was still with her. Mari sweetly smiled and took in the message.

Later that week when the press tour was coming to an end, Mari told me that she had heard that it was on my itinerary to go to the Samurai cemetery on Sunday. I acknowledged this to be a fact. Mari said that coincidentally she was going to be there on Sunday, due to the fact that it was her family's burial site as well. In addition to that, her uncle's memorial was being held that Sunday at the same time that we were going to be there. We were both a bit stunned by that fact, but also strangely amused, because we both knew that we were being brought there together for a reason. After all, there are no coincidences; somebody's always pulling the strings.

Sunday finally arrived like a long anticipated friend showing up to meet us. Fumi, our animated host, escorted us to the cemetery, and he wasn't sure what to expect. He probably thought the ground would open up and swallow us all for my even thinking about communicating with the Samurai. It was a majestic site full of history with an air of importance and beauty. The day was warm and lovely with a slightly ominous feeling in the air. Joe and our girls were expecting just about anything to happen, as they had traveled with me often and knew that I was a tour guide for the past.

We barely entered the grounds when a petite Japanese woman came running towards us seemingly frantic, waving her arms so furiously that even Fumi was taken aback (and he at least knew the language she spoke). We were at a disadvantage and felt like we were being rushed by a small woman with a message and a wild look in her eyes. I thought somebody needed the Heimlich Maneuver or something, so I was prepared for an emergency situation to be thrust upon us. Judging from her demeanor, there was something urgent going on. It turned out that the woman was the wife of the head priest, and she knew Mari very well, so she was wrangling us in for tea and cookies. Mari had told her in advance that we were coming. Wow! Both a relief and a surprise. We were happy to oblige.

We barely sat down when Mari walked in, and I stood to give her a hello hug. We thanked the kind woman for her generosity and embarked on our stroll through the headstones of the 47 Ronin Samurai. "Ronin" means "they are without a lord to follow."

We purchased some incense to burn for the Samurai, and

my girls were very comfortable taking part in this ritual. It was a multi-faceted experience. It was really sad that the Ronin Samurai had died in such a way, at the same time the honor and valor that they displayed were admirable. It was one of those moments where you want to "take a knee" and bow your head, but you can't put into words why.

I asked Joe and the girls to give me some time alone, so that I could absorb the feeling around the Samurai and write the impressions that I got in the cemetery. I closed my eyes and placed my hand on a large headstone. I saw a Samurai appear on a horse, and he pointed up above the Ronin cemetery further up a hill. He told me that all of the Samurai were not with him, some of the family were missing, and they were up there. I also got the impression that they may have been buried before up the hill, so I wasn't sure if they were up there or not. It was a little confusing to me.

I know some of you might wonder how the Samurai could communicate with me, since he spoke Japanese. I think he, too, had someone on the Otherside acting as sort of an interpreter, making it possible for me to understand him. I know when very young people die, I have to ask an older generation to help bring through the child. They sometimes have to speak for them or "lend them" their energy, so that would be a sort of interpreter situation. Also, the dead can make me feel what they felt, and they are capable of showing me visions of what happened to and around them for me to put into words and relay to the living, which makes me a sort of interpreter myself.

The Samurai showed me a vision of women falling to their knees in the streets, sobbing and begging for their men back.

The Samurai told me that they died for political reasons, and that they didn't have to die. He said that they were "the guardians of the temple," which I took to mean the Buddhist temple on the grounds. As Joe and I were leaving the cemetery, I told Joe that my stomach hurt pretty bad, and I felt nauseous. Joe explained that when the Samurai died, they did so by disembowelment, and that could explain my stomach pains.

So we continued to a museum on the grounds where they housed the actual chain armor and relics of the Samurai. The girls were walking around taking in the history and the beautiful relics. Then my oldest daughter came up to Joe, complaining of "stomach pains"—not a big surprise. After a brief explanation to her, we set out to see the second museum on the grounds.

We reconnected with Mari and her cousin as we walked through a museum that had sculptures of the 47 Ronin Samurai. I pointed to the one that had on a uniform that looked like the one the Samurai on the horse had been wearing. Mari was taken aback by what I had said. She took it in and explained that the particular outfit that I had pointed out was the one worn when the Samurai take their life when sentenced to death. It's seen as honorable. Also, in order to be a Samurai, you have to be born into the clan, so it's also seen as their duty.

I shared the rest of the Samurai information with Mari, and she told me that before they avenged the death of their slain lord, the Samurai had divorced their wives and left their families to try and save them from political, as well as social persecution. One Samurai even courted and married the daughter of the architect of the enemy's palace to gain the blueprint of the palace for the attack. Another Ronin Warrior acted as a drunk who was always at the local pub. He was often spit on by villagers for being a disgrace to the Ronin Warriors.

When the Samurai had ultimately carried out their vengeance, and their families realized the sacrifice their men had made for their lord as well as their family, the women were beside themselves. This would account for the vision the Samurai showed me of the women falling to their knees. One of the men who spit on the drunk Samurai impaled himself out of shame for doubting the warrior's honor.

We walked back to the office where we had begun our tour with tea and cookies, and I thanked the priest's wife for her hospitality—in Japanese of course: "Domo Arigato!"

(I had picked up a little Japanese through all of my interviews, and a book called Japanese for Dummies.)

Mari then asked the wife if she knew the answers to the rest of the Samurai statements to me. The petite, lively woman didn't, but stated that there was a groundskeeper who had been there longer than she had, so they summoned him. He was a wonderful energy. He felt like a combination of the earth and sky, grounding yet full of dreams and possibilities. He was very helpful, and said that there were three members of the Samurai clan who were still buried up the hill where the Samurai had indicated earlier. In addition to that, he said that long ago all of the Samurai had been buried up there and later moved to their memorial. Everyone else was floored. I was just glad that I had conveyed the messages clearly. I'm a stickler for that, and getting confirmation on our information kind of scratches an itch for mediums.

I know that I am not the only person who has interacted

with the Samurai since their tragic yet noble deaths. Think of all of the children who have walked the same steps that I have. They see what I see . . . they just aren't always heard. "Hey mommy! Look at the Samurai in the green uniform."

"Yeah honey, that's nice. Hurry up now."

So, if you are a parent, listen up, because kids often have messages. Remember, it wasn't so long ago that it was thought impossible for a man to walk on the moon or to have a phone without a chord . . . not so long ago. After all, it's what the eye hasn't seen, but the mind has created, that becomes a reality that had been there all along.

When we left for the airport to go back home, our girls were misty-eyed. They had grown so attached to their security guards and Fumi. They loved Tokyo and they wanted to stay. I couldn't blame them—it was an extraordinary place. My two youngest talked about the giant beetles at the toy store that Japanese children buy and watch wrestle their friends' beetles. Yes, REAL beetles, and yes, they play with them like toys. Wow! I love being immersed in different cultures. My daughters also drank a lot of tea and participated in the Japanese Tea Ceremony, learning mutual respect.

It's customary in Japan to bring a token of respect to the people you visit, even something small. We brought Arizona Wild West Sheriff's badges and Arizona trivia books, things like that, and they received them as though they were the Hope Diamond. We received from them origami cranes and frogs, candles, etc., and we appreciated the sentiment. We also have a new respect for bowing to pay respect to those around you.

Our hotel room overlooked the Tokyo Tower, and it was

marvelous. We got a chance to see the sun turn red, just like on the Japanese flag. It was breathtaking. People who can travel should see as much of the world as possible. It changes your perspective on how you think and how you see others. In fact, my trip reinforced for me that we are all given the chance to be feeling beings, and when we exercise that part of ourselves, there are no barriers between us. Language barriers are not so hard to overcome in life or death, as long as you learn to interpret.

Years later I asked Joe, "What would the world be like if everyone believed in life after death—if everyone was open to communication?"

While in Japan we noticed most people were Buddhist or believed in honoring their ancestors, knowing that spirits remain around us. They were not smug, or arrogant. It felt so light there, so accepting. Then I came home and the energy was so different. I wouldn't have known this if I had never gone there.

In some areas in the world people just want to be right or win an argument. They have no belief system (not an internal one anyway), an inner navigation system, if you will, or an unbreakable spiritual connection to one another—and that's a crying shame.

Each and every country exudes a different sort of energy, and unfortunately, we seem to lack cohesion in our country. Our energy is a little "scattered"; nobody seems to fully agree on anything.

After 9/11 there was a brief time when we stood united behind our flag. I think we were all proud to be Americans; we were secure in our unity and the American Spirit. Now, we have people who hide behind religion and picket our soldiers' funerals, the same soldiers who fight for their freedom. It's so despicable. I never thought I'd see freedom be so abused, but it happens on a daily basis.

I hope for more for my children's generation, that there will be less hate in the world and fewer people to judge them.

I always tell my kids that it's healthier to be around people who will allow you to be true to yourself, not individuals who will try and make you into another version of themselves. Our girls "get it," and they embrace being interesting kids. What they learned in Japan will always stay with them. The experience has definitely made us all better people.

Chapter 9

Bad Acts

People often ask me, "How many murder victims have you brought through?"

I don't know the answer to that question, sadly. I lost track a long time ago. That sad fact really struck me, after one of my events where I brought through a woman's young daughter who had been killed by a family member. I had to ask the mother if the male cousin had killed himself, because the case sounded so familiar to another reading I did that was practically identical. In this case, the killer didn't commit suicide. He was in jail, and that was the only detail that let me know I hadn't read this woman before.

I still don't know how people who take someone's life selfishly can live with themselves. That would torment me every day of my life. I'm sure for those who kill and find their conscience through "Jesus" while in jail, the memory of their crime must eat them up from the inside out, realizing the enormity of their actions. At least I hope so. I tend to sympathize with the victim, not the perpetrator. I never understand people who are more concerned with the criminal's feelings rather than the victim and their family. I'm not one of those people.

I think we've become desensitized through movies and television to people who are murdered, because we see it all the time. So I decided to share the stories of the real people who lose their life, so that you never forget them. This chapter is an effort to open people's eyes to murder victims, so that you recognize that they, like you, had a pulse; they had a life, and they all matter to someone.

We need harsher laws/penalties and more enforcement of them, but that's for another day.

It's hard to explain to somebody why people kill… there are different motives behind taking a life, whether it be possessiveness, hate, war, money—whatever the reason, they all result in death, which leads to a memorial, mourners, flowers and a finality that leaves loved ones asking themselves "Why him?" Or, "Why her?" And sometimes, "Why MY baby?"

Jereme

I meet many people who lose their family/friend to murder, and yes, it takes a toll on me. How can it not? Anyway, I was in Phoenix, Arizona, at one of my events, and I met a young man named Justin Privett, who wanted to hear from his brother who had been murdered. Justin looked like the kind of young man who doesn't enter arenas like mine often, but he looked willing and eager, so I was up to the challenge. He also looked like, under other circumstances, he would be a great deal of fun to know personally.

My first impression of Justin was that he was a very strong person who was in a lot of pain. Pain that he was trying to both understand and attempt to rid himself of. It's always hard reading a young person, because sometimes information comes through that has to be confirmed by an older generation. I was hoping his guard wouldn't be up, because that makes my job somewhat harder. When a person is read, they're already a little "deer in the headlights" because their grief is causing them stress, and it makes it harder for them to process the information that I'm giving them in the reading.

When Jereme came through, he was cool and edgy with a wicked sense of humor. He talked about his brother, Justin, having three tattoos in memory of him. But during the reading Justin forgot about one of them, thinking he only had two. He later shared with me that there were in fact, three. Because I know that people often freeze up during a reading, I knew that Justin's brother was right, so I didn't even flinch when Justin said he had only two tattoos. I just continued forward with his reading.

Justin was actually more receptive than I had expected, and he seemed to "get it" more than most, because he knows his brother's energy and knew this was his "best friend" in the room. He appeared to be able to sense Jereme, too, because they were so close. The reading became more complicated when I said, "Your brother lets you know he's around by messing with wires and electronics." Just then the fire alarm and lights started flashing in the ballroom, so I had to continue trying to concentrate on the messages with a few minor distractions. The audience understandably gasped, and a couple of people actually exited the ballroom. I thought that was sort of amusing, but they came back when they were less "spooked."

Jereme's Brother's Story

I first heard of Allison DuBois through a mutual friend, who is a prosecuting attorney.

She also happened to be the prosecutor on my brother, Jereme Lee Privett's murder case. Allison came up in a discussion I had with her after a status conference in downtown Phoenix regarding my brother's murder. We were in the hallway of the courthouse discussing up-coming court dates and so on, when she brought up her friend (Allison) and told me the story about the jury that was deliberating for a long time (this not being good for the prosecution). She told me about Allison's prediction on when the jury would return a verdict. I jokingly asked her to "call her friend and ask her the outcome of my brother's trial, so that we would know the result without all the worry and stress!"

"First contact with Allison DuBois"

My Aunt Thel (Thelma Vivian) called me in early January of 2010 and told me that she had bought two tickets to an Allison DuBois conference for that month, and she asked me if I felt up to going with her. She later told me she had been nervous to ask me to go with her, not knowing how I felt about this "sort of thing." I told her I would love to go, as we have both lost a number of people close to us lately, and so I thought it would be very interesting to see. (My mother, Bonnie, passed in March of 2007. She was Thelma's second sister to die young.)

We arrived early, hoping to get ahead in line and be seated close to the stage. We were both surprised at the small personal setting that the conference provided. By my count, there were about 220 people in attendance. The first four rows were VIP sectioned off by a red velvet rope two rows in front of Thelma and me. Allison began with a witty introduction and described her ability and how she uses it. Inside, I was a little bummed thinking that if this lady starts doing these awesome family readings, that only the VIP people were going to get the hook-up. I was wrong. I was the first audience member on stage.

"My reading from Allison"

After a short introduction, it didn't take long for Allison to jump right in and start her thing. I was shocked to be selected first to be asked on stage in front of everyone with Allison to "make a connection" with a loved one. As a skeptic having never done this before, I was a little nervous. Not because of the crowd, or my eyes already welling up with emotion, but because I didn't know what to expect.

We introduced ourselves by first name and I had a seat next to Allison. She asked the relation of the person I wanted to contact. I responded, "brother." She then picked up a yellow legal pad from a small table between us covered with about thirty neatly arranged #2 pencils and a box of tissue, and began to write my first name, and the word "brother." She said, "Give me a few seconds," as she sat focused on the pad of paper and a square box she was tracing over again and again. Allison gave a little chuckle with a smile and said, "I've got him."

My brother and I are 4 1/2 years apart, me being the oldest of my mom's only two children. We grew up together very, very close, always sticking together, never being separated from each other for more than a couple of days at most—all the way through adulthood (minus my 4 years in the US Navy). We shared apartments together as adults, owned a business together, a boat together... like I said, very close. We even had a regular "40 Night" once a week on my porch, where we would just sit outside, smoke cigs and drink 40 oz. beers discussing the week, friends, girls, business, all of the fragments that construct a life.

After the chuckle, Allison said... over and over, "Bro the man, bro the man...." He keeps saying 'Bro the man.'" His cell phone attachment to my number was "Brodaman." NO one knew that. Next, she pointed out three tattoos that my Brother thought were awesome that I got for him in memory of him. None were visible on me; they were covered by my clothes. On my left ribcage I have the same tattoo as my brother. It's the Privett family crest done after he passed away. Seth Rowan, a close family friend did the artwork for the tattoo on Jereme shortly before he died on one of our trips to Oregon. I also got that same tattoo months after my brother passed away by the same hands. It's very special to me. Next, I got a large "OE" (old English) gangster-style tattoo across my stomach. It reads "BROTHER." Third, I got an old cowboy-type "Wanted" scroll tat on my right rib cage that was similar to the one on my chest that simply says "in loving memory," with my brother's full name and a big "83" for his birth year. These tattoos, all three of them, were UNSEARCHABLE... she nailed this on the head. Pretty cool.

The third thing she said was that she was being showed how he died. She pointed to the correct side of the back-side of her head, tapping it, and she said, "He keeps saying, 'cheap shot, cheap shot...100% accurate.'" Then, not even knowing the situation, told me that Jereme said he could hear me talking to him when he was on the ground.... This is odd because she could not have known that I was there, nor that I was digging blood from his ears telling him how much I loved him as he lay dying. All this was just in the first 30-45 seconds. Allison read me for over 8 minutes.

A lot of what she said was personal, so I choose to keep it to myself. I'm sure you can understand that. Allison then stated that my brother could get my attention by messing with electronics. The next thing you know the fire alarm went off... LOUD! I had a handheld microphone. She was wired, and no one could hear us now with this loud alarm going off, not to mention the flashing lights. Allison looked at me and told me that this was memorable and asked, "You know that's Jereme, right?" To which I nodded "yes," with big tears in my eyes. So, the audible alarm shut off within a couple minutes and we moved on with the bright warning lights from the fire system still blinking.

A number of other pertinent things were communicated to me by Allison, all the way down to the odd music I selected for my brother's wake... all punk music. After all, he was young. Now we've all heard "Amazing Grace"... so I picked Transplants, Pennywise and Offspring. He was 25 years old—it fit.

After the many cool things Allison brought up from Jereme, it was time to move on. She asked if I had any questions for him. "I've got a million. I will limit it to one cuz, there are a lot of people here that want to meet you."

So I asked about my brother's remains and what he

wanted me to do with them. Allison smiled. After a second or two, she made it clear that my brother was saying this jokingly... he was showing me driving one of the cars at high speed and dumping his ashes dusting all the other cars on the freeway! Totally what I would say if I was the stiff. She knows my brother.

I stepped off stage and as soon as I hit the bottom stair, the emergency lights shut off. So frickin' weird! Now I pop light bulbs everywhere I go. It kind of sucks, yet still I know it's because he's beside me and always will be . . . a small price to pay for his company.

As a footnote, Justin let me know that the person responsible for his brother's death was indeed convicted of First Degree Murder. A small measure of justice for his family that will hopefully save someone else's loved one by taking criminals off the street.

Lindsey

I get to meet a lot of people touring. It's one of the perks of my job. Some events are heavier than others, depending on the cause of death and the age of the victim. The energy of my audience varies, depending on what city I'm in. In June of 2010, one of my events was in San Diego, California. During my meet-and-greet I met a family of four women who all wore T-shirts with a picture of a little girl on it with the word "MISSING." The mother explained that her ten-year-old daughter had disappeared almost a year ago, and they had no answers. Their pain was palpable and their anguish was visible in their eyes. I have a little girl the same age as her daughter Lindsey, and putting myself in their shoes, I would do ANYTHING for answers, too.

I took the stage, and this family was in the front row. I was absolutely going to do whatever I could to help them move forward one day at a time. I brought the aunt up on stage and made sure they wanted to hear whatever I picked up on, because you never know what will come through. She nodded in affirmation, so I put my pen to my pad of paper and began to scribble. I began sensing the man who took Lindsey, and a young female energy was giving me the information that saddened me. As I suspected, it was their Lindsey. I felt like she was immediately removed from the scene in his truck, and I did not feel she was alive any longer.

Lindsey showed me some details involved in her crime that I passed onto the family for the police. The little girl said to assure her mom that the detectives and the officers took her abduction very seriously, so much so that sometimes they can't sleep at night wondering where she is, so she was in good hands with them. The little girl then said her mom wore something around her neck for her, and the mom confirmed this. She then said she wanted to go to Disneyland. The family gasped because they were debating whether or not to go the next day. The mother said she didn't want to go when her Lindsey never got to go. I said, "Well, she wants you to take her. She says she'll go with you tomorrow, that you can go together."

She talked about how loved she felt by her family and shared other details. Then I concluded the reading by saying, "I'm going to break my connection with her and send her with you."

I then began my next reading, but I had to stop. "Um... Lindsey's singing "Somewhere Over the Rainbow" in my head, so that's the song that will let you know that she's around you. I then shifted my energy back to the new reading. Lindsey's mom left the ballroom to collect herself. When she came back she said, "I don't mean to interrupt, but when I was in the lobby just now "Somewhere Over the Rainbow" came on through the speakers. "I thought I was going crazy, but there it was."

I responded with, "She's letting you know that she's really here beside you, and in a very good place."

That was a truly touching moment for everyone there that night. Not too many dry eyes in the house, including mine.

Lindsey's Aunt's Story

My great niece, Lindsey Baum was a sweet and vivacious 10-year-old at the time of her disappearance (on the evening of June 26, 2009) from McCleary,Washington, a small town of only 1400 people. She was walking home from a friend's house a short distance from her own home when she vanished without a trace. On July 7, 2010, we will be celebrating another of Lindsey's birthdays without her. This will be her 12th birthday.

In May of 2010, ten long and agonizing months after her disappearance, there were still no solid clues leading us to her. Something needed to happen, and so in our quest for answers as to her disappearance and to FIND "Our Angel, Lindsey," we sought out the help of renowned medium, Allison DuBois.

We first checked Allison's website for information about contacting her and found that she would be in San Diego, California, on June 2, 2010, as part of her "2010 Family Connections Tour." We promptly purchased VIP tickets for the seminar which allowed us to attend a pre-event "Meet-and-Greet" with

Allison. Four of us, including Lindsey's mother, Melissa Baum, flew from Seattle, Washington to San Diego, California for the chance to see and possibly capture the attention and ear of Allison DuBois.

We did not know what to expect, but only hoped that our encounter with Allison would provide us some sort of answers to Lindsey's disappearance. If we could come back with one tidbit of information, the trip would be worth it, yet in our minds we had no idea what to really expect.

When the session began, we were immediately taken by the young, vibrant woman that entered the room. She exuded an energy and passion for her gift, and upon our first encounter, she seemed to already be in touch with our purpose for being there—finding answers to our Lindsey's disappearance. It seemed to us that Allison already had an awareness, as if she knew that she was coming to speak to us about Lindsey, and as if it had been in Allison's mind in advance. That is how keen we perceived Allison's abilities to be.

Allison's specialty is helping connect people to missing children with the intention of helping to locate them, and so she announced at her introduction that she WOULD begin with Lindsey. To our amazement and obvious pleasure, we had succeeded in reaching Allison! We were ecstatic beyond belief.

Living in the time that Lindsey has been missing has been a surreal experience in itself, but on this night with Allison, our emotions and anxieties were higher than ever, and we felt a different kind of surreal feeling connected to this unique experience. Allison was calm and centered in her approach and gave generously of her time. She spoke with precise and distinct knowledge of things that no one except someone with her unique gift could ever know to tell about. We were awestruck by the words she spoke so knowingly of Lindsey and who she is, the little girl she had never met.

If you have any information on the disappearance of Lindsey Baum, please contact Grays Harbor County information hotline (tip line) 866-915-8299.

No psychics please, as you can imagine it overwhelms their phones. Witnesses and people with direct knowledge of Lindsey's disappearance only, please.

Tori

I was traveling to Canada on tour when I struck up a conversation with a very likeable gentleman sitting one row back across from me on my flight. We took turns bragging about our kids. His happened to be on the flight, and I could see why he was so proud of them. It was a lengthy flight, so there was plenty to talk about, including what we do career-wise. I hesitated, because I don't like to talk about only my life, and trust me, that is exactly what happens when people find out what I do. I, on the other hand, enjoy hearing about other people's experiences, since I'm quite familiar with my own.

He ended up being very cool about what I do, and as it turned out, he was a constable in Canada. At some point, he began telling me the sad story of a little girl named Victoria Stafford who had been missing for a few weeks. I always try and help when I can, but I'm also aware that I am simply one person, and I have time limitations in my schedule, just like everyone else. He gave me his card and told me that he hopes that I "feel better." I had a touch of bronchitis, and had seen better days. I was in Canada on "tour" for book signings, as well as my lectures that I'm known for. I had three or four events in five days, so it was a bit grueling, and as I had said before, I wasn't 100% physically.

My manager, Mark, and I stopped to get some fast food that was underwhelming per usual. I reached for the door handle, and as I looked up, I was met with a paper stare coming from Victoria Stafford's "MISSING" poster. I got a sick feeling in the pit of my stomach that morphed into a constant pang of guilt.

I said to myself, "Boundaries, Allison! You can't help on every missing person's case you come across. There will be no time to breathe!"

Still, there was something haunting about Tori's eyes, and the image of her wouldn't leave me. We left, and Mark and I mapped out our week down to the minutes we would have to eat along the way. I dropped Airborne like it was my oxygen to live, trying to jumpstart my immune system and make it through my first event, and I did! Whew, what a relief. All the while I was thinking of Tori and all of the people who were hoping for her safe return, since there was speculation that she may have been sold into sex slavery. What a horrendous thought! Still, it was better than some of the alternatives. What a crippling, sobering reality is that? I'm a spiritual being, but I do believe there are some people who should pay a higher price for their crimes than society sees fit.

"Mark? What if we swing by Woodstock (Tori's hometown)

on our day off?"

He smiled and replied with, "I'm game."

So we drove the 45-minutes to Woodstock to the scene of Tori's abduction, coincidentally right across from her elementary school. We meandered down the main fairway passed town signs in front of hotels and restaurants reading, "Bring home Tori!", "We love you Tori", "Give Tori back to us!", letting the abductor know that they'd called out the whole town and they had a fight on their hands, because this baby was precious and was parented by the entire town now.

My being in Woodstock started to feel very personal, as I saw the wounded town awaiting the return of their missing child. Tania, a friend of mine, was familiar with the area, and we followed her to the school that Tori had been last seen leaving with a woman. I yanked out my pad of paper and pulled up a chunk of curb to park myself on, as I concentrated on the moment Tori went missing, to try and get some clues connected to her disappearance. I wasn't even sure I'd get anything, quite honestly. I had been so sick and my energy was low.

The first word I scribbled was "Alive?"

Answer: "No."

My heart sank—that sucked! So now I knew we were looking for a body. I couldn't get emotional, I had to continue writing.

Question: "Motive?"

Answer: "Sexually motivated." Not good. I felt the female was just a lure to get Tori to go with her, and that there was a male who had planned this all out to assault Tori. I also felt that the perps "knew" Tori's mom. That was a very important piece of information. Also, that the male had a tie to the neighborhood;

he either lived there or had a close connection with someone who lived there. I saw trees around Tori, like the woods or an area where you might camp. The male perpetrator was familiar with this desolate area. I also felt like the female was trying to get information from neighbors to find out what they knew, and may have attended a candlelight vigil that I found out was being held that very night. The only real good news is that I "knew" they'd be apprehended and that Tori's body would be recovered and returned to the town that held her so close to their hearts.

Woodsy areas are vast, so when I sift through my information, I try and pull the pieces that can lead investigators to a direct connection with the perpetrator. For instance, I knew the male perpetrator had a tie to a female that lived in Tori's neighborhood, and his mom and/or girlfriend live really close to Tori. While I was picking up on that I could also feel that the male and female knew Tori's mom personally, meaning they've come into contact with Tori before. An interview with Tori's mom then becomes a great source of finding out who did this to Tori, knowing that she has met her daughter's killers.

I slowly began to rise off the curb, a different person from when I sat there earlier. Now having the answers that I told the constable I'd call him with, I had the answer that everyone searched for, and I felt sick about the information that I needed to share. I hesitated to call him for a moment, wanting to let five more minutes of hope exist in everyone's mind.

I rang him up and, of course, his first question: "Is she alive?"

"I'm sorry, no, I don't feel that she is."

You could feel the hope vacate his body, I believe confirming what he already felt in his heart to be true. I filled him in on the other details and somberly hung up. A couple of months later, Tori's body was discovered by a search party and brought back to her hometown. She was in a woodsy area all that time where she had been waiting to be found. Another beautiful little girl taken from us by monsters, and sadly she won't be the last.

When I'm driving, I always look at the faces of the people in the cars, searching for signs of distress by something other than rush hour. You know to see signs that they're being "transported" unwillingly, just in case you could place an emergency call on their behalf or recognize a child from an Amber Alert. Once a child is kidnapped and transported on a freeway by their captor, their chance of survival drastically drops—so keep your eyes open out there.

A couple of unsettling statistics for people to keep in mind is that boys between the ages of six and nine are the most highly abducted and murdered of males under eighteen. Girls around the age of eleven are the most highly abducted and murdered of all children under age eighteen. So, even though kids want to exercise their freedom, keep those statistics in mind when letting them go anywhere alone, even three houses down. I've see it too many times to count where they were just walking a few houses away. Food for thought.

A year would pass before I would return to Canada for another event.

I had just finished two events in Rochester, New York, and my cousin and I sat in a sports bar in Niagara Falls watching Mark's San Jose Sharks play ice hockey on the big screen, while we waited for our ride to Canada. When Wendy, our ride, showed up, she had a newspaper in her hand and she looked somewhat irritated. I was in a good place, hanging out with my cousin watching ice hockey in the town my husband was born, and I was through with two events, so I was halfway home.

Wendy placed the paper on the table in front of me and the front page read, "I Knew Tori Was Dead," with my picture next to it, and Tori's, as well. I felt like I'd been slapped in the face by a giant. I was smiling in the picture and I found that disturbing, because I would never look happy about something so dreadful—it was certainly in poor taste. I have a lot of trouble working cases under the radar; if I comment on a case at all it can be turned into a front page story. Anyway, I've been in so many magazines, I'm surprised I haven't married Bigfoot yet (at least according to them)! My sense of humor is all that pulls me through sometimes. It's a rough world out there, so take it with a grain of salt people!

On the Hill

Many think that I reside in a bubble unscathed by murder. First, let me say that every case takes a toll on me. How could it not?

On July 19, 2010, I was awakened by a police officer's voice saying (and I'm paraphrasing), "Do not come out of your homes—we're releasing the dogs!" This was a stone's throw from my bed, and I was in that groggy state that allows you to go right back to bed, especially since I had a cold. So sleep was all I wanted to do. When I awakened, Joe was noticeably shaken.

"What's wrong?"

Joe replied, "One of our neighbors was stabbed to death this morning and the police have blocked off all of our streets. The killer's on the loose still."

There was very little information released at the time about the victim. The killer was said to be a male, medium build. "Well, that narrows it," I thought.

There was a police car parked right outside our house, so I felt fairly safe and sure the killer was no threat to my kids. I started pondering the thought that someone was the last person to talk to the deceased, and didn't realize it, and someone was now standing in the presence of a murderer, and was unaware. "How frightening," I thought. You never really know what kind of person you're standing right next to, what they've done in life, or who's handing you your burger at the drive-thru window. Have their hands pulled the trigger of a gun that took a life?

We live in a neighborhood with armed guards that's considered "ultra-safe," and still bad things can happen. I knew this, but sometimes a reminder comes in handy as to not take each day for granted. I've sat in courtrooms and watched the killer's family cry for them just as hard as the victim's family, and it brings certain conflicting feelings to the surface for me.

We are all human and we make mistakes, some much bigger than others. In the end, whether we live in fear or ignorance (most fall somewhere in between), it won't change the outcome of how our lives end, but rather changes what we create while living. If you live in fear, you go through life basically holding your breath and turning your power over to those who want it; so in the end you never truly lived at all. If you live in total ignorance, chances are you will foster someone around you to walk a line that most likely breaks rules and ignores consequences; and that's not fair to those who play by the rules.

A killer never forgets looking into the eyes of the person they victimize, but the deceased lets go of the killer as soon as they die. It's the family/friends that are now in the position to identify and stare down the person who robbed them of their loved one.

What a sad day it was in my neighborhood. I prayed for the man who died and his family, because no matter what safety bubble we think we live in, we're all affected—because we're all connected.

As a footnote, the murder suspects were quickly apprehended; it appeared to have been a love triangle that ended tragically.

Chapter 10

Not Forgotten

I was doing a show in Las Vegas, and I started talking to a man who puts together USO tours for Iraq, and he asked me if I would ever consider going. I said, "of course," and then I started thinking what could I possibly do to lift their spirits (no pun inten-ded)? I don't sing or play an instrument, I can't strut up and down a cat-walk—what's my talent? I talk to the Dead.

"Wow, that will really help them!" . . . I thought in my most sarcastic tone. I'd probably be a "walking taboo" to the soldiers, someone to fear because I'm so close to death—the very thing they're trying to avoid. I can't say that I blame them if I somehow seem taboo to them, being too close to tragedy all the time.

So, even though I never heard from that man again, he did get me thinking about ways to give back. I did still want to do something in tribute to our soldiers and their families for all of their many sacrifices.

My dad was a marine in the Korean War, my brother was Army Infantry in Nicaragua and recalled for Desert Storm, my Uncle Joe was in the Navy. Many, many of my family members have stepped up to the plate, so this topic is very close to my heart.

I've also have brought through a number of soldiers from WW II, Vietnam, Desert Storm, and our current war in Iraq. This is my way of reminding us all to never forget what they did for us. So this is my small contribution to the men and women who are the fabric of our flag. We are deeply grateful for all that you are and do!

While sifting through the e-mails from the parents who lost their children to war, I found it difficult to choose one. But this one stood out for me because it struck me that there are various ways to lose a child to war, because they leave shards of their soul behind in the battlefield.

James

One of the e-mails that I got was from a woman named Debbie, whose son James, had died tragically after serving our country so valiantly. Her 30-minute reading was set for March 23, 2011, and I was geared up to deliver a very meaningful reading for James' family.

Debbie was a very bubbly, appreciative lady who clearly loved her son and wanted to connect with him.

I started. "James says he's not the only "James," there's another one."

Debbie responded, "Yes, his father's name is James."

I continued, "He shows an open road and a Jeep. He likes to go on road trips with the wind blowing through his hair."

Debbie shared with me that her daughter got a Jeep after James died.

No doubt he rides as the co-pilot in his sister's Jeep.

The next piece of information he gave was he wanted to acknowledge the birthday in JUNE.

Debbie came back with, "James' sister's birthday is in June, as well as his nephew's."

He talked about his pictures being all over the computer, and he told me to ask his mom about the necklace that she wore for him.

Both were confirmed. The necklace contained his ashes.

James said one grandfather had passed and he was with him. He said to tell his mom to take out a picture of them when he was five-years-old, because that's how he wants her to remember him.

James then screamed the name NICK in my ear, so I asked Debbie who Nick was to James. She sniffled and said, "Nick is his brother." I let her know that James said that Nick wouldn't have believed in the reading had he not been mentioned by name. She laughed and confirmed that to be true.

Debbie asked for messages for family members and brought up his two nephews. One was named Nico, she said. He was exactly like James, his very image. I inquired as to how old they were and she said, "Eleven and five."

"Debbie, did you put it together that James said that he appears five-years-old now, and his nephew, who is his spitting image, is five-years-old? "

We both sat there for a moment and took it all in.

Debbie had shared that like other mothers, she carried the guilt to have not been able to save her son or "make it all better." All parents can relate to this. I did remind her that sometimes the ability to "save" is taken out of our hands, and that guilt and grief seem to go hand-in-hand. We must find a way to let go of the guilt to lighten the intensity of the grief. Grief still affects us, but it's more mutable without guilt, so it can be investigated and processed by all who experience it.

I concluded my reading with Debbie and she graciously thanked me. I thanked her back for sharing her son James with me and my readers, so that we can know both how wonderful a son and soldier he is. Plus, his reinforcement that family is indivisible—even by death.

"Debbie on her son James"

As a toddler, James was so pretty that once a woman said to me: "A boy? He's much too pretty to be a boy."

When he smiled, his eyes would twinkle like the stars. His face would light up like the sun, and it was then you saw his dimples.

He was the little boy everyone loved. He was the little boy who was not afraid to speak out about what his eyes saw in the world. You never knew what to expect from him; he was silly and spontaneous.

I remember feeling my heart melt as I saw the world through the eyes of my child when at age 4, James proclaimed, "Look around, isn't it a beautiful world we live in?"

Growing up, James was small for his age, so in his teen years his size earned him the nickname of "Shorty."

I don't think I ever heard his friends call him by his given name. James was also very sensitive to others' feelings. When he was 19, I came home to find him waiting on the steps for me. He pointed to the garden and said, "The cat got your favorite squirrel, Mom, so I made him a little wooden cross and buried him cuz I knew you would be upset."

That's the sort of "sweet" my son James was to me.

It was after the Twin Towers tragedy that James decided that he wanted to join the Army. I tried to talk him out of it—me being a 1960's "peace and love" Mom.

He said, "What if no one served, Mom? I will be doing something good for someone else."

My son was in the service for six years. He was a soldier who suffered with depression.

I will never forget the night the police came to tell me about my son. It was bitter cold that day and it was about to get even colder. It was midnight when the police rang my doorbell.

"Hi, are you James Allen's mother?" they asked.

"Yes, I am. Is something wrong?"

They responded, "There is no easy way to say this . . . your son has been found in a hotel room. He's dead. It's being reported as a suicide."

Just like that! The words riveted through my skull.

"No, I'm sorry, but you're wrong. That can't be my son. My son is not even in New York!

He is in the military, and he's out of state."

"Ma'am, we found his ID in his wallet. That's how we knew to come here."

My mind raced. "Well, someone must have stolen his wallet!"

I felt sick as if none of what was happening to me was real. This can't be. It's a joke, a sick joke! I went to the phone. I needed someone to tell me what I knew to be true: James would never do something like this to himself or his family.

I called his siblings and I repeated over and over, "The police are here. They are saying your brother killed himself . . . but you know James would never do anything like that, right? You know that, right? It is all a mistake. You'll see in the morning when we go to the coroner's office."

The next morning on the way to the coroner's office, I remember praying as my husband drove the car. I don't think it really sunk in until I walked into the room and saw my other children sitting there. It was the way they looked at me that made me start to back up as I pointed to them and said over and over, "No, No, No. This is not true!" Then the wait, and begging God, "When they raise the curtain, please don't let it be my son." Over and over I begged. All the prayers in the world could not prepare me for what I was about to see . . . .

I remember him lying there behind that glass. "He looks cold," I said. "Can I get him a blanket?"

I really don't know what I was thinking. I just remember feeling sick—a kind of sick that I've never experienced before in my life. It was agony. I went outside to throw up in the snow, and all I felt was numb. A piece of me died that day with my son . . . and my world would never be the same.

I have four children, each one different. James was one-of-a-kind. In his eyes, I could do no wrong.

For me, there are no more notes from him, each one ending "xoxox James."

For me, there are no more "I love you, Ma" at the end of every phone call from my loving baby boy, James.

Debbie's Story

I had always believed in life after life, even before my son's passing. Now that he had passed, it wasn't enough to just believe. I had to buy and read every book I could get my hands on about the subject. One of my favorite books, and the most comforting was Allison's book, *We Are Their Heaven*.

I needed to learn as much as I could if I was to continue my relationship with my son. I needed to connect with him.

There was no note from my son. There was no closure for me until the first time I met Allison at one of her seminars.

My daughter raised her hand to ask a question. Allison started to answer her, and then said, "I'm sorry, I need to stop you there."

It was then she turned to me and asked, "Are you the mother? Because I have a message for you."

As long as I live, I will never forget that day or the words that followed.

Your son said, "You need to stop thinking the way you're thinking, it's not your time." He also wants you to know that he IS a mama's boy, and always will be a mama's boy.

Simple words to some, but for me it was the first time I had heard them from my son. Those were the very words his brother used to browbeat him with when he was younger: "You're a mama's boy, mama's boy!" as James would hug me and look at his brother to irritate him even more. To hear those words from Allison gave my heart joy, something I hadn't felt in some time. She followed up with a few more messages from my son, and when we left, even my girls were believers at that point.

"You were right Mom, its real. Allison is the real deal! That was our brother. Oh my God, we heard from James!"

We all cried that night, but this time it was tears of joy that we shared.

To have Allison do a read for me in depth, a second time, was more then any mom could ever hope for. It was a blessing from God.

There are no words to describe the emotions I felt as she delivered message after message from my son.

"Debbie's Phone Reading, 2nd time she had spoken to me"

She started by describing my son with the "wind in his hair" on a road trip in a Jeep.

"Why does he keep showing me a Jeep?" she asked. At first, I could barely answer. The joy in my heart was overwhelming.

James' sister had bought a red Jeep in memory of her brother, because he said he had always wanted a red convertible. She had the tire cover painted with James' life years and name, honoring his memory, and would take the top off and ride all over the place in her jeep. She insisted she could not get rid of it, because her brother loved it. She was right.

First, confirmation from Allison as she continued to tell me he loved riding around with his sister in the jeep.

"He keeps saying, "Ask my mom about the necklace."

"Do you wear a necklace for him?"

Every day since the day after his funeral service, for more than three years, I have worn a necklace with a cross on it that carries my son's ashes in it. When Allison said that my son knew that, for the first time in three years I felt at peace just hearing that.

The only time she mentioned any names was when it came to James' brother, Nick.

She said, "He also references a "Nick" connection to him. Do you know who "Nick" or "Nicholas" would be to your son?"

Nick is James' big brother. Nick does not have an open heart in matters of life after life.

After delivering James' message for me to give to Nick, Allison said, "It's funny, his brother wouldn't have believed if I hadn't come through with his name."

Allison had no clue that Nick was a nonbeliever. As if the rest was not confirmation enough for me, to have Allison say that just about knocked me over!

She relayed many messages. James even had advice for his sister, Carrie, about her current situation at hand. I know my son James is still with us, that he loves us and he knows we love him more than words can possibly express. My son was so proud of being a soldier, and we will always honor him.

"Tribute to James from his mom"

Love is the tie that binds us together forever. Death is not the end, it is a new beginning.

YOU BATTLED THE DARKNESS UNTIL
YOU FOUND THE LIGHT. XOXOX

SPC James Patrick Allen
April 3, 1982 - February 8, 2008

Chapter 11

Team DuBois

It's been six years since we first filmed the pilot for Medium (March 2004), and so much has changed since then. We were informed in October 2010 that after seven seasons of unbelievably great writing, producing, and acting, that MEDIUM would take her final bow in the United States in January 2010. A lot of people told me how sorry they were that it was ending, and that's so sweet. I was fine with it coming to an end, personally. I am a real person, and it's hard to be compared to my character all the time. It was kind of funny, though, some of the things people would say to me: "Allison, why doesn't Patricia have red hair?"

(Well, because she's a blonde.)

"Allison, do you really talk to dead people?"

(Uh, yeah, that's why the show centers around a woman who talks to the dead.)

"Allison, does your house look like the one on the show?"

The questions were endless, and I understand people's curiosity. It's just that sometimes you want to have regular conversations, and now I can do just that.

We had seven wonderful seasons, and I met a lot of great folks along the way. My daughter, Fallon, became very close to Maria Lark (the actress who portrays her), as did we all. She's like a fourth daughter to us. I got to know the mysterious Glenn Caron and see his genius create a show that will be re-membered forever. Patricia Arquette (who I've always said is a "much softer version of me") is inspiring to know because she really does want to help make the world a better place. She's so fantastic. Jake Weber, also a wonderful human being. And Ladies, does he play a great husband and dad or what?

Anyway, as much as I love the show, it was great to go out in the #1 slot for our time period. Going out on top is preferred. So, I was fine with the show coming to an end; I could embark on a new phase in my life.

Writing this book, for instance, is very important to me—so is touring, creating new shows, and figuring out what I want to change in the world with my family by my side. Every time I go on tour, my kids seem to grow another inch, or make a memory that I wasn't there to witness. Now that they're older, I can take them with me when I travel and show them the world they were born into. Even though they share me with the people who need my guidance, they will always be my priority, and now is a good time to remind them of that fact.

I've learned a lot being in the spotlight. There's a lot of criti-cism when you're a public figure, and people are waiting for you to fail. But as long as you're true to yourself, their opinions of you don't matter. I'm a medium, and we're expected to lead a boring, mundane life, and just be around to answer questions—but you know we're more than that.

I've always been an explosive redhead who's loyal to a fault, and I'm very passionate, and guess what? I have a social life and I like to have fun with my friends, and I won't feel bad for that. Some people would like me to fit into an "image" of what they think I should be, but I'm going to live for myself instead. There's a lot of pressure for everyone to be what others WANT you to be. Don't give in to it.

Honestly, the mediums whom I know are an unpredictable blast, and talented, to boot. We immerse ourselves in death all the time, so when we're "off the clock," we just want to re-join the living and revel in the life that others aren't here to enjoy. Mediums tend to be a lot of fun, actually, and I'm so blessed to know many wonderful, gifted people in my field.

Joe and I have been together for almost twenty years. We have created a colorful, exciting life side-by-side, and I can't wait to grow young together. Our daughters are developing into lovely young ladies, and each one of them is remarkable and one-of-a-kind.

Joe and I moved to Los Angeles, California a couple of years ago so the girls could spend more time with me while I balance a career and my incredible family. We feel connected to our new friends here, and we still have a strong bond with our friends in Arizona.

I am passionate about touring and writing, so needless to say, I will continue to do both for a very long time.

The words in this book are meant to educate people and further the mending of broken hearts everywhere.

"When in the midst of loss and despair, remember the spark of life can never truly be extinguished."

– Allison DuBois

Acknowledgements

I want to acknowledge some courageous, spectacular people who have touched my life as well as my family's life. I'm so grateful to have been graced by them all.

Bill Austin, who passed in 2010 from a terminal illness. He was the morning show host on *Beth and Bill* - 99.9 KEZ in Phoenix, AZ. He had an infectious laugh and he touched too many lives to count.

Michelle Stark, who passed in 2010 from cancer. She had a beautiful voice, an angel's face, and a husband and two daughters who adored her.

Dr. Jim Hayes, who passed in January of 2011 from pancreatic cancer. He was truly a loving, intelligent human being with a great golf game, to boot.

Elvia Van Es, who passed from a brain tumor. She had a lot of spunk, and was a shining star. She reminded me of the best parts of my dad's family, so she felt sort of related to me—comfortable, like family should be. She loved margaritas and most especially, her family. Only the good die young, right?

Deidre, my nephew's mother was full of young, radiant energy and was extremely thoughtful, always writing me thank-you cards. She died in a tragic accident. I know she'll love and protect my nephew, Michael, and his little brother—always.

Obviously, thank you to my handsome husband, Joe, and our three gorgeous girls whom I couldn't live without. They've endured this roller-coaster ride with me, and they still have a sense of humor.

Thank you to my mom, Tiena, who reminds me that all that matters is what a person thinks of himself or herself, and that you can't live your life for other people.

Jaena - You're like a sister to me. Thanks for your friendship and never backing down.

Thank you to Patty and John S., Amy Berberich, Tania Thomas, Patty and Chris Flores, "Juke Kartel" (Toby, Tommy, Dale, Jay and Todd), Terry D., Tom McMullan, Rodney Smith, Draden Medina, Dr. Ole Alcumbrac, Mary Grassl, Rich Berra, Tim Hattrick; my friend/attorney, Josh Binder; my publicist, Valerie Allen; Adrianne Curry, Steve Stark, Pat and Duffy, and all our friends in Pinetop, . I went through a moment of introspection recently and you all were "there for me," and accept me for who I am. There are no words. Thank you.